Anonymus

The Two Bishops

A Tale of the Nineteenth Century

Anonymus

The Two Bishops
A Tale of the Nineteenth Century

ISBN/EAN: 9783742831248

Manufactured in Europe, USA, Canada, Australia, Japa

Cover: Foto ©Andreas Hilbeck / pixelio.de

Manufactured and distributed by brebook publishing software (www.brebook.com)

Anonymus

The Two Bishops

THE TWO BISHOPS.

A Tale of

THE NINETEENTH CENTURY.

LONDON:
Catholic Publishing & Bookselling Company, Limited,
CHARLES DOLMAN, MANAGER,
61, NEW BOND STREET, & 21, PATERNOSTER ROW;
DUBLIN: J. MULLANY, 1, PARLIAMENT STREET.
1860.

AS A TRIBUTE TO

The Cause of Truth,

THESE PAGES ARE

OFFERED BY

THE AUTHOR.

Rome,
May the 1st, 1860.

PREFACE.

In the following pages, the endeavour has been rather to trace conscientious convictions to their just conclusion, than to attempt a record of historic facts or actual events.

The Author has glanced at the follies of a system, in order that, under colour of fiction, it may be more forcibly proved, to all earnest minds, that a search for Truth must result in submission to the Unity of Faith — " the One Church Catholic of Rome."

THE TWO BISHOPS.

CHAPTER I.

FRANCIS and JULIAN VAVASOUR were the sons of a rich and highly-born gentleman, who had died whilst the two young men were completing their education at Oxford.

Francis, the elder, was intended to hold the family living of Lillyfield; and Julian, much against his inclination, was destined for the bar.

The sudden death, however, of their father, released the latter from his promise of not selecting his own profession, and opened out a path to a life more in unison with his own feelings.

That there is a greater evil to be overcome than poverty, in all its varied sufferings, he felt the more assured, the more he pondered over the spiritual destitution of his native land, so apparent even within her proud colleges, and in spite of her many public institutions for the education of her children. During his sojourn at Oxford, often had Julian endeavoured to discover a remedy for a state of things which, to every thoughtful mind, must appear a great national evil.

In that time-honoured seat of learning he saw science carried to perfection. The wisdom of this world seemed to be attained by all. And not as mere scholars had Oxford good reason to boast of her sons: they were also finished gentlemen, whose elegant tastes exercised as much influence in the fashionable, as their more solid acquirements in the political world. But in the signs of the times Julian saw a striking resemblance to the 18th century in France; when a school of philosophy arose which summoned to the bar of Reason the most sacred truths, and rejected those which could not stand the test; when the spirit of rationalism pervaded every class of society, and men were found to call in question even the sublime and consoling doctrine of the soul's immortality! Turning over the historic page, he marked how many disciples of this school had been, at the hour of death, forced to acknowledge that mere human learning was but folly, when not employed in extending the teachings of Him whose wisdom is farther above the comprehension of men than the heavens are removed from earth!

CHAPTER II.

FRANCIS VAVASOUR rapidly ascended from the family living of Lillyfield, through all the various dignities of his sacred profession; and now, thanks to his great talents, and the extensive political influence of his father-in-law, the Earl of Burtonfell, he has been named as the Bishop of ——

It is the season of 1851, and London is filled with the *élite* not only of England, but the world. The Great Exhibition has accomplished what nothing else could do—it has united men of every shade of opinion. For a time, the Utopia of "Liberty, Equality, and Fraternity," seems on the point of being realized! Perhaps only one requisite is wanting to make it the grandest spectacle the world ever saw; and that is the golden chain of universal faith!

Lady Blanche Vavasour, the wife of the Lord Bishop of ——, was the only child of the Earl of Burtonfell. Idolized by her parents on account of her extreme beauty, she had been accustomed from childhood to make her will their law. When, at eighteen, she had chosen to fall in love with the handsome rector of her father's parish of Lillyfield, she found no difficulty in obtaining her parents' consent to the marriage.

Brought up from her cradle to regard herself as a beauty *par excellence,* she grew up in utter ignorance that any mental discipline was required for her. And yet, in addition to being considered the *belle,* she was pronounced "the most accomplished young lady of the season." At the time we introduce her to our readers, if she was, without comparison, the most elegant woman in London, it cannot, I fear, be denied that she was one of the most worldly of Fashion's daughters. Her greatest trouble at this period of her life was the extravagance of her only son, a captain in the Guards, and the obstinacy of her daughter Marion, who would not be convinced that a season in town was absolutely necessary if she ever wished to be considered *crême de la crême.*

Picture to yourself, reader, all that you could

ever imagine a beautiful woman to be, and your ideal will fall short of the matchless, glorious beauty of Marion Vavasour! From her mother she inherited her slight, elegant figure; but there all resemblance between them ended. No pen could portray the surpassing loveliness of that face, or convey the expression of holiness and purity in those large violet eyes. When a little child, the villagers of Lillyfield were wont to say "that they seemed to gaze upon an angel as she passed by."

Faultless as she was in mere external beauty, far more was she in the hidden beauty of the soul. There were deep feelings in Marion's heart, for which the worldly society in which she moved could hardly have given her credit. To herself, it often seemed as if she had a dual existence. There was an inner chamber in that pure, fresh young heart, into which she shrank, with almost a sense of pain, when she thought that even her mother could neither share nor understand the feelings it contained.

Lady Blanche Vavasour was essentially a woman of the world, who lived for fashion and society. Of the working or poverty-stricken inhabitants of London or ——shire she knew little, and cared less. They were "those tiresome people" of whom she sometimes heard statesmen speak, when dining at her father's table. She passed them in her carriage in the crowded streets — pale, careworn women, — gaunt, half-starved men. And yet she gave her money freely to any public charity. But, as she used to say, "those people were not of her *monde*. There were churches for them, and they would not attend. What more did they require? If they liked, they could get work; but they preferred leading an idle life. Well, it was not *her* fault." And so the subject would pass from her mind.

Far from our wish is it to portray Lady Blanche Vavasour as a type of her order. Such, thank God, is not the fact. Among the highest ladies of our land there are not wanting those who prove, by their daily lives, that *they*, at least, consider the care of the poor a most sacred charge.

Unlike her mother, Marion was deeply interested in the condition of her poorer brethren; and often did she ask herself why it should be so difficult to win their hearts, and obtain a certain control over their minds? She frequently asked herself whether this had always been an obstacle? There must be, she felt assured, some cause for such an effect.

She heard a great deal about the "Church," and the increasing divisions among its members. And here, again, the poor were blamed,—"they would rush into Dissent."

Deeply as Marion respected her father's opinion, she could not conceal from herself the fact that the Holy Bible, which from childhood she had heard called by the members of her Church the ground of their faith, alluded, in express terms, to there being "one Lord, one faith, one baptism." But, among her co-religionists, where is she to find this unity?

A few months since, and the highest legal tribunal of the land decided that each one might settle for himself the important question of baptismal regeneration! Again, some there are who deny the Holy Trinity. And they, too, proclaim themselves Protestants; and, what is still more lamentable, they have but exercised the right their religion accords to them "of judging and interpreting the Bible for themselves."

She hears her father preach, from a text of Holy Writ, doctrines that are stoutly denied by the clergyman of an adjoining parish! If both preach the faith "once committed to the saints," why should they not agree on the smallest as well as the most important points of doctrine? In the material world all is order and subjection; surely an equal harmony ought to be conspicuous in the spiritual world.

CHAPTER III.

It is midnight in London; and who has resided in the modern Babylon without being able to realize some of its horrors? Who is there, when returning in the well-appointed carriage from the opera or the ball, who does not, sometimes at least, shudder on passing through its brilliantly-lighted streets, at the contrast between themselves, rich in friends and the comforts of home, and the droves of wretched creatures who have no refuge save the streets and the gin palace? Reeling from the latter, many are consigned to the tender mercies of the police, and pass their night at the station-house. Others, mad with despair, rush to the fatal river, and, thinking at one leap to end their miseries on earth, awake too late for repentance, and find themselves in the hands of avenging Justice!

Oh fearful thought! While the votaries of fashion and pleasure are absorbed in the fascinations of the ball and the opera, bright and immortal souls are perishing in our streets! Many of them, stricken with remorse, would fain at once turn from their evil ways. But where, or to whom can they apply? They are homeless, friendless. Not one ray of hope dawns on their souls. On the one hand, the demon of suicide beckons them to destruction. The other alternative is a slower, but equally certain death of soul and body.

Oh! ye noble daughters of England, placed by a kind Providence high above want and its temptations, look with pitying eyes on your fallen sisters! Spare from the abundance at your disposal sufficient to enable those who are working in this holy cause to open refuges throughout London and elsewhere, whose doors will at once unclose to admit the wretched applicant! Suffer no distinction of creed to stop the current of your charity. Think of the powerful aid you can render to the servants of the "Good Shepherd." In His name they are seeking the "lost sheep," who, vile and repulsive as they seem to you, are still dear in the sight of Him who died that they might live.

Listen not to the falsehoods uttered against the true friends of virtue, the pure, good nuns; but, oh, believe that noble, delicate women, as they are, must be actuated by some holy motive in devoting themselves to the rescue of the lowest of their sex; and that the only reward they hope for is the salvation of immortal souls.

In one of the lowest alleys of St. George's Fields, in a miserable cellar, utterly devoid of furniture, save a wretched bed, if such it could be called, and one broken apology for a chair, were assembled, as the Cathedral clock chimed the midnight hour, a group of persons whose varied appearance would have raised the astonishment of many of those young and noble ladies who probably at that moment were the centre of attraction in some splendid drawing-room of aristocratic Belgravia. Kneeling before a rusty grate, endeavouring to coax an obstinate glimmer of light into a cheerful blaze, was an elderly woman in the dress of a Sister of Mercy. Her efforts were at length rewarded, and the fire burnt up, and threw its cheerful, ruddy glow on that miserable room, lending even to it an air of comfort that had not been felt for many a long day.

Carefully unpacking a large basket which stood beside her, Sister Mary Joseph—for so she was called—proceeded to take from it a kettle and tea-things. Having placed the former on the fire, she quitted the cellar for a few minutes, and returned, accompanied by the mistress of a small shop near, of whom she had begged the loan of the tiny table and chair which they carried between them. The next thing was to make the tea; and having placed on the table a new white loaf, and some fresh country-looking butter, the worthy sister, with a face beaming with good-nature, called the attention of the other two inmates of the cellar to the attractive display it made.

Lying on the wretched bed was a young woman who had probably numbered some two or three-and-twenty years. Her face was pale as marble, and round her faded blue eyes might be seen a deep-sunk line of black. It was by no means difficult to perceive the traces of former beauty, and her manner clearly proved that she must have once occupied a very high position in life.

Old and threadbare as was the black dress she wore, there was not wanting that indefinable elegance in the wearer, which, at the first glance, established her title to the name of " lady." The delicate white hand, which hung feebly by her side, gave token that she was of gentle blood. The soft low tones of her voice were of themselves sufficient to persuade even an uninitiated ear that the speaker was not an ordinary person. And such the heart of Mrs. Tichborne (another lady present) felt assured she was not, from the first moments those sweet accents fell upon her ear.

To explain how it was that these persons found themselves assembled in that mean apartment, it will now be necessary to relate occurrences that had taken place some hours previously.

CHAPTER IV.

BRIGHTLY burn the candles on the altar of the Most Blessed Sacrament in the noble cathedral of St. George's Fields; for, it is Thursday night, or, as the poor Irish of that neighbourhood would tell you, "Sure, it's Benediction night." Kneeling amid that crowd of Christ's poor was one figure which could not fail to attract the attention of even an utter stranger to the ancient faith. It was that of a slight, elegant old lady, of some seventy years. In her youth she must have been very handsome, for she still bore the remains of former beauty. It was not alone the mere beauty of feature that was so remarkable, but the kind and intellectual expression of that face. Time, with his iron hand, had stamped upon that noble brow lines which death alone could erase. The occasional quiver that passed across the delicately-shaped mouth, told a tale of intense suffering that had extended over many a year of trial and anguish. But the expression of the soft dark eyes, as they rested lovingly on that wonderful token of her dear Saviour's love, was that of one who, having cheerfully, for His sake, taken up a heavy cross, has in the end found peace. Such, indeed, had been the fact with Mrs. Tichborne. Friends, children, husband, all had been snatched from her in early life. Blessed with ample means, she now in her old age devoted her time and fortune to visiting the sick and afflicted, and comforting the widow and the fatherless.

Few were the miserable hovels in the densely-populated neighbourhood of St. George's Fields, where she was not a constant and most welcome visitor. Poor "artists and artistes," struggling clerks, poverty-stricken sempstresses, sick governesses, broken-down ladies and gentlemen,—to all these, in turn, was Mrs. Tichborne most truly a "ministering angel." Nor was it a mere expenditure of money: she displayed a far more refined and exalted charity in the kind sympathy with which she entered into all the feelings of these despised ones of earth, and the delicate tact with which, more especially to the unfortunate of her own class, she would cause them, even while receiving her alms, not to feel oppressed with the sense of obligation.

She was, on the evening of which we write, kneeling in her accustomed place, not far from the altar of the Blessed Sacrament, when the sweet notes of a most exquisite and plaintive voice, singing, as though it was a cry of agony from a broken heart, that beautiful petition of the Litany of Loretto, "*Consolatrix afflictorum, ora pro nobis,*" arrested her attention, and caused her to look at the singer, who was kneeling at her side. It needed not the thin pale face, down which tears were rapidly flowing, the almost transparent hands, clasped, as though in mute appeal to her whom she thus addressed, to convince the warm heart of Mrs. Tichborne that here was a fresh object for her benevolence. Her eye had just fallen upon the wedding-ring on that slender finger, and the thought flashed across her mind that the earnest suppliant was perhaps a widow, mourning for the husband of her youth. But then, she wore no garb of widowhood. Could she be, and the idea pained the kind old lady, that most miserable of all creatures, an ill-used and unhappy wife?

All other sorrows can be told to the sympathizing ear of a kind friend; but, let the domestic trials of a wife be ever so great,—should her heart be torn and bleeding from the unkindness and neglect of him whom she has loved better than father, mother, or aught on earth beside, it can only be when her husband's conduct has crushed her very spirit, that the lips of the tortured wife are unsealed!

The beautiful service had ended; the last joyous notes of the "*Laudate Dominum omnes gentes*" had died away; the candles on the altar were one by one put out—all, save the bright red light which ever burns before the Blessed Sacrament, and still that youthful figure, with head lowly bent upon her upraised hands, knelt like a statue, save that a gasping sob from time to time escaped from her. At length, a gentle hand was laid upon her arm, and Mrs. Tichborne whispered, "Follow me to the sacristy."

What passed between those two it is not for us to reveal. Suffice it to tell, that at the close of a somewhat long interview, during which the sufferings of many months had been confided to the sympathizing ear of Mrs. Tichborne, the lady quitted the cathedral, in company with two Sisters of Mercy from the adjoining convent, whom Mrs. Tichborne had instantly summoned to her assistance. The whole party were conveyed in the carriage of the kind old lady to the miserable room where we first made their acquaintance.

CHAPTER V.

The presence of so many kind faces, after having been so long utterly friendless, proved too much for the object of Mrs. Tichborne's care; and, on being lifted from the carriage, she had fallen into so deathlike a fainting-fit, that for some time the doctor, who had hastily been summoned, hesitated to say whether she would recover from it. From the first moment of seeing her, he declared that she was sinking, from actual starvation! As he positively forbade her removal, Mrs. Tichborne instantly despatched her carriage and servants to —— Street, Grosvenor Square, with orders to bring an immediate supply of food and blankets.

With one deepdrawn sigh, the eyes of the poor sufferer slowly opened, and in soft low tones, and an accent which told she was of foreign birth, she gently murmured, "Oh, if in the past dreary months I had but known you, dear lady, what anguish would have been spared me! How little did I ever dream, in the sunny days of my youth, that I, my parents' darling, after being for awhile a husband's idol, should be deserted and forgotten by him! Yes," she went on (clasping Mrs. Tichborne's hand between her own poor thin ones), "there was a time when he did love me. For him I quitted the joyous land of my birth, and exchanged the bright skies of beautiful France for the leaden-hued ones of your smoky London. His love for me threw a charm over every spot, and to be with me made all places alike to him. But soon, alas! I observed a change in my husband's manner towards me. He became cold and harsh; he removed me from the pretty cottage to which he had first taken me, near London, to a dingy lodging in the city. He hinted darkly at his being in difficulties as the reason for this change, and finally spoke of the necessity of going to his father for assistance. He told me that none of his relations knew of his being married,—that they had been absent from home at the time of his return to England,—that now it was essential he should visit them. One day, having given me a small supply of money, he bade me adieu, promising soon to write and to return. Weeks passed without my either seeing or hearing from him, and I was in utter ignorance of his address. No shade of mistrust had crossed my mind that it was his intention to desert me; my only dread was lest he should be ill. Day after day I waited patiently, in the hope of receiving some intelligence, but in vain. At last, being no longer able to pay my rent, I received notice to quit, from my landlady, and suddenly found myself alone in the streets of London, without a friend to whom I could apply, or a roof to shelter me!

"I am an orphan, and therefore had no parents to write to, even had it been in my power. The few things of value which I once possessed had all been seized for rent. I walked along in a state of despair rapidly bordering on frenzy, when I was accosted by a poor woman whom I had sometimes relieved.

"Utterly friendless as I was, the sight of this poor creature afforded me comfort. I told her my misfortunes, and she at once took me to this miserable abode, where for some days she has most kindly shared with me her scanty meals. To-night I accompanied her to St. George's Cathedral, intending, by her advice, to have asked assistance from the kind priests, who are ever ready to relieve the sufferer.

"Whilst kneeling before the Blessed Sacrament, I cared not if the hearts of all mankind should close against me; for I well knew—and joy and peace came with the thought—that there was not one among all my sorrows with which the sacred, loving heart of Jesus did not sympathize. And, oh!" she continued, "how can I ever be sufficiently grateful to Him for having sent me a guardian angel! Had it not been for your kindness, dear lady, I might, even amid the abundance of this great capital, have died, as I hear many have done, of starvation!"

A pause of some minutes followed the close of poor Violet's melancholy tale. At length, Mrs. Tichborne kindly said,—

"Well, well, dear child, great as your trials have been, they have proved a blessing to you. I have often," she continued, "in my anxiety about the future, been comforted by the reflection that He who cared so much for the 'lilies of the field,' as to bid us look on them as examples of His loving providence, will not permit any of His servants to perish." And she softly said, whilst her eyes filled with tears, "no gratitude is due to me for my poor services. I am but a humble instrument in the hands of our great Master. A brighter future," she cheerfully added, " is yet in store for you. One night more, as we have arranged, you remain in this poor home, and then you remove to mine. These good sisters, who will tenderly nurse you, will tell you better than I can of the humble birthplace of our adorable Lord, and the lowly home of Nazareth, where for thirty years He was pleased to dwell. I shall come early in the morning, and fetch you myself."

And having given some directions to the worthy sisters, and kissed poor Violet's pale cheek, Mrs. Tichborne quitted the room, and was soon in her carriage, and once more on her way home to —— Street, Grosvenor Square.

CHAPTER VI.

A CLOSE observer might have detected a shade of care on good Mrs. Tichborne's brow as she sat musing on the events of the day, previously to retiring to rest. Often, indeed, had she mixed with those whose daily lives were one long course of suffering. But deeply as her kind heart felt for the poor creature whom she had just left, there was another reason which caused her, inured as she was to misery in its worst forms, to shudder when she thought of Violet.

Strange and wonderful events are by no means of unfrequent occurrence; and we need not seek far in search of a living drama of such absorbing interest that all imaginary details will fall short of the actual realities of life. We often pass, in the crowded thoroughfares of London, individuals whose lives, could we lift the veil which covers them, would actually furnish us with the materials for such a drama. But we see the exterior deportment only; their hopes and fears, joys and sorrows, are alike unknown to us.

We have been led to these reflections by the extraordinary revelation made to Mrs. Tichborne in the Vestry of St. George's. Often had the simple tale of suffering been enough to call forth her charity. But never before had any case appealed so irresistibly to her heart. In the course of her narrative, Violet had mentioned the name of her faithless husband. As Mrs. Tichborne was connected closely with his mother, neither he nor his family were, of course, unknown to her;

and already a scheme presented itself to her benevolent mind, which the perusal of these pages must develope.

Some perhaps may think that in thus taking into her confidence and home a perfect stranger, Mrs. Tichborne proved herself sadly deficient in that prudence which a seventy years' acquaintance with the world must have imparted to her. But having heard from poor Violet the name of the priest in France who had performed the ceremony of her marriage, any doubts that might at first have entered Mrs. Tichborne's mind were at once removed. For the Père Jean was wellknown to her. Only the summer before she had visited the little village where his cure lay, and he had been a welcome guest at her house. Any information, therefore, which she might require regarding the marriage, could easily be obtained.

She was by no means ignorant of the difficulties which might beset her in her attempt to establish the validity of the marriage in question. And if successfully proved, before a legal tribunal, how must the heart of the wife be pained by the necessary exposure of her husband's guilt?

"No," said the kind and considerate old lady;

"there is another way of endeavouring to arrange this sad affair, and it shall be my task to discover and carry it out."

CHAPTER VII.

Speed from the vast metropolis of England, through a bright and pleasant country, such as our own dear land alone can show! Quickly we leave behind us pretty villages with their quaint old churches, standing half-concealed by ancient trees. We catch a passing glimpse of brown, honest faces, upturned in astonishment at the "express train" as it shoots past them. Then comes a refreshing perfume of new-mown hay. Hours glide on, and still the fiery iron steed holds on his course.

At last a change is visible in the scenes through which we are hastening. Tall chimneys, black with the accumulated smoke of years, send up a lurid light towards heaven. The faces of the people bear an unhealthy hue, telling, in language without words, a tale of dark and dangerous mines, where, deep in the bowels of the earth, the sons of toil wear away their lives.

Nor are the hours thus spent in labour the darkest portion of their lives! Think of the night, when these coal-stained men, emerging from the pits with minds ignorant of anything like pure and holy thoughts, seek their sole recreation in brutal pleasures, intemperance and vice!

Ah, ye philanthropists! and ye who talk so much of sending teachers to some far distant land, think ye no heathen sits in darkness in our own?

The years during which we have lost sight of Julian Vavasour have not been idle ones to him. On leaving Oxford he had entered a Catholic college.

For this act of his soul's conviction he was, of course, denounced by his brother and all his relations, who "having done all that was required of them by declaring him an apostate, and forbidding him their houses," on finding him resolved to continue a Catholic, were content to leave him alone.

Julian, dearly as he loved his relations, experienced only a slight vexation from their conduct towards him. He thought far more of the thousands of immortal souls perishing for lack of some kind hand that would break and distribute to them the bread of instruction.

Humbly, though zealously, working in the cause of his great Master, he devoted all his energies to the cultivation of that portion of Christ's vineyard committed to his care. And now, to the sorrow of his entire flock, the dearly loved " Father Julian," is removed from his humble mission at ——, to the important position of Catholic Bishop of Branston. But here no grand palace received him as its master; and sure we are that at his death no newspaper will proclaim to the world that he saved from the poor of Christ some hundred thousand pounds!

It is not in the splendid drawing-rooms of the great, or in the magnificent House of Lords, that you must go in search of *our* bishop. No; you must seek for him rather in the wretched home, the miserable cellar, where poverty and fever have struck down their victims. There you will find him, communicating to that dying soul the Holy Viaticum that is to support and cheer him during the last stage of his earthly pilgrimage; or he will be met on the "highways and byways," in search of the "lost sheep," bringing in the "blind and the lame," whose bitter lamentations had reached even to the throne of the Most High—"No man cares for us." There, in fine, where death may come from the very air he breathes, where sin reigns, as it were, triumphant, does the faithful pastor carry the standard of the cross, and plant the glorious banner even upon the citadel of the great enemy of mankind.

The time of his coming to Branston was one of great sickness. Cholera was daily, nay hourly, carrying off its victims. The energies even of the medical men seemed to be completely paralysed—"All," they said, "that human skill could do, had been tried in vain to stop the awful scourge in its deadly course."

The state clergy, too, had in many instances followed the example of their terrified parishioners, and fled with their wives and children. "It was," they urged, "the sacred duty of a husband and a father to provide for the safety of those dearer to him than his own life." Alas! they altogether ignored the perishing souls thus left to their fate!

But in the plague-stricken hovel, by the side of the poor dying sinner, at any hour of the day or night, might be seen one man wiping the death-sweats from the ghastly face, and soothing the horror-stricken soul with the consolations of religion. Yes, wherever cholera raged most fiercely, there was the Catholic Bishop, Julian Vavasour! He seemed to have no thought of self, and never appeared to fancy that he was doing more than his duty in thus exposing his own life for the benefit of these strangers. No difference of creed prevented his rendering all the assistance in his power to the rich or poor in Branston. They were, he said, fellow Christians, and in visiting the "sick," he but obeyed his Master's command.

But, alas! when the hand of the avenging angel was stayed, and time had healed the wounds which the loss of so many loved ones had made, the remembrance of all that the good bishop had done for them was forgotten by the many, who seemed to think that the fact of his being a Catholic was sufficient reason for refusing him their gratitude!

There is heroism in mounting the breach under the cannon's deadly fire. And well deserve they their country's warmest thanks, who, gallantly leading the charge against the enemy, fall beneath the standard they have given their lives to save! But there are those who have won their honours in the cause of suffering humanity, and performed far more heroic deeds, and yet no voice is raised either to cheer or reward them!

Ah, well! there is an eye which never slumbers, and a record is faithfully kept of service done in His name who never leaves unrecompensed the " good works " of even His humblest follower.

CHAPTER VIII.

Branston had once been a very agreeable place to reside in; but this was at a period when its society was far less tainted with that vice of evil-speaking which, alas! in this boasted age of "progress," is to be found rampant in every town and village.

Branston society had become divided into three parties or cliques. There was the "Low Church," the "High Church," and what may be considered a mixture of these two. They were not exactly "Dissenters," nor quite "High Churchmen."

At the head of the Low-Church clique was a Mrs. Major Smith, who, having as she felt convinced, secured her own future welfare, through the "ministry" of her favourite pastor, the Rev. Jabez Raile, had a considerable amount of spare time; "and," said the worthy lady, "how could I better employ it than by placing myself at the head of a committee of ladies, organized under the able guidance of our beloved shepherd, for the 'total destruction of the Church of Rome.'"

Though the said Church had so long contended against the assaults of Protestantism, that had vainly dashed herself, and broken into a hundred fragments, against this "Rock of Ages," these deluded individuals felt assured that her final overthrow was now on the point of its accomplishment, and through their means!

But, there is a difficulty yet to be surmounted by the various parties into which the Protestant system is now divided, and which the members of this committee, in their zeal to "convert the Papists," appear to have overlooked. They appear to lose sight of the fact, that in the Holy Catholic Church there is perfect unity; and, therefore, the first thing that would alarm the mind of an apostate from that Church would be, the absence of this unity amongst any of the denominations of Protestantism.

What, then, are the consequences that commonly follow apostacy? The unhappy individual, seeing no reason for giving to a new faith the obedience which he is now instructed that he must not render to any form of Church government, avails himself of this "liberty of conscience" to become, first, a free-thinker, and finally, an infidel.

Little did Mrs. Major Smith imagine that such might prove the sad result of the monthly meetings held at her residence.

It was the night for one of these gatherings. Mrs. Major Smith was in the chair, and grouped around her were several of her cronies, one of whom, a Miss Stellard, we must beg to introduce to our readers.

Miss Stellard was what may be termed a religious "touter;" a woman of tremendous energy, to whom nothing came amiss. Did any of her party propose a new association, no matter for what object, from a workshop for furnishing garments to naked little Indians, to the formation of the Branston Ladies' Society, "for the total extinction of Catholics all over the world!" to assist in any of these good works, Miss Stellard was ever at her post, or, in other words, in the drawing-room of her friends. Thus, according to the time of day the committee sat, she contrived to refresh herself with the various delicacies of the house and season.

"And what is the good news for this month?" began Miss Stellard; "I have not yet had time to look at the *Convert's Chronicle.*"

"I am thankful to say," replied the chairwoman, "that this month's number contains matter which will prove deeply interesting to us all. There is the account of an old woman who has renounced her pestilent errors, and the revelations she has made of the horrors of the Confessional are really worth your perusal."

"Oh dear me! how very nice," exclaimed Miss Stellard; "I am so anxious to know what those questions are which Papists are asked. The perusal of them will indeed be a treat to us all. But," she continued, "I met with such an adventure yesterday, it is quite a mercy that I am here to relate it."

"What was it?" echoed all the ladies; "did you meet the priest, and did he attack you?"

"Oh no, dear friends," laughed the amiable lady; "not quite so fearful an encounter as that would have been. No; the fact is, I had occasion, during my district visits, to enter the cottage of a woman who has lately withdrawn her children from our school, and, seduced by bribes of some of those rich perverts, has sent them to that den of iniquity, Union Street. I had taken the precaution to carry with me a basket of tracts, and had been reading to Mrs. Guest that sweet one, 'The Papist in Flames,' when I suddenly discovered (and here the speaker's voice sank to a whisper, and the curiosity of the listeners was wound up to the highest pitch) an old woman ('a female Jesuit!' screamed the ladies) sitting behind the screen, which had prevented my seeing her before. I immediately asked her why she did not send her children to school. Imagine my horror when the creature informed me that children she had none, for she was a single woman; but if she had, it was to the Catholic school they should all go. 'And 'tis a Catholic I am, and the siven generations before me. Proud is Judy O'Sullivan to own herself that same, my lady.'"

"What a plot of the Jesuits," said Mrs. Major Smith; "no wonder that so many lambs are stolen from the fold when concealed Papists are to be found even in the dwellings of the poor."

Little recked these mistaken ladies the numbers of persons to be found, even in their own town, who, in the enjoyment of all the privileges of a state-supported establishment, with its army of clergy, were, sad to tell, sitting in the darkness of the heathen! Some amongst them were of the highest class in society—men of wealth and education, who attended church on Sundays, as a mere outward conformity to the rules of the world, but to whom the words of the preacher were, by themselves, never supposed to apply. Surely not to them who attended in their handsome carriages, and gave their cheques for the charity sermon, could those strong denunciations against sinners be directed. The poor man who, in a moment of dire want, steals a loaf of bread, is summarily and severely punished; while the rich lawyer, who has robbed the widow and the orphan, sits in his well-lined pew, and sleeps! Ah! sleep as he may do now, the still small voice will one day assert its right to be heard! But, in the mean time, no "society" calls upon him to repent and make restitution; no "mission" is sent to waken him from his spiritual death.

Here, for the present, we take our leave of the "Branston Ladies' Society," assuring our readers that we have not overdrawn the characters of any of its members.

CHAPTER IX.

THE evening chosen by Mrs. Major Smith to assemble her committee was one on which the Catholic bishop of Branston was to conclude a "Retreat," or course of spiritual exercises, given for the benefit of a number of those poor artizans of whom we have made mention.

Oh ye who differ from the ancient faith, but have human hearts to feel, for once throw aside your dislike, enter with us into the despised Catholic Church, and listen to the holy truths which that faithful servant of Jesus is teaching to that vast multitude.

Beautiful as is the language in which his discourse is clothed, sweetly as those accents fall upon the ear, it is not these alone which stir up pure and holy thoughts in the hearts of those who hang with rapture on his words.

Hush! he is speaking of the life to come; telling these poor despised ones of earth that with true penitence they, even they, may one day hope to enter heaven.

He comforts them, though tears are falling fast from eyes which never until now, perchance, have wept at the remembrance of their sins. But life, new life was opened up before them, and, in their inmost hearts, they feel that a master's hand has struck a chord which thrills within them. The words they listen to come warm from the soul of him who is addressing them. Swifter than travels the electric spark, their souls receive the welcome message of good tidings from the kingdom of Him who is the very God of Love.

A solemn stillness pervades that vast crowd of Christ's poor. There is something almost awful in the silence which prevails. Each soul seems bowed in humility, in order to recognize the presence of Immortality, as, taking in his hand the image of our crucified Lord, the bishop, still speaking of that better, holier life, the one to come, bids them remember, as they look upon that sacred symbol of their redemption, that not only must they strive to follow His divine example, by submitting to trials and sorrows here below, but when they think of Him, the "sinless one," to bear in mind that none can enter heaven with one stain of sin, for all is pure and holy there.

Oh! thought to make the boldest heart amongst them quail! But one of hope, as well as fear, to all who have entered on the narrow way of the Cross!

The pale rays of the moon, streaming through the stained windows, seemed to form an aureola of celestial light around the bishop's head, as, turning towards the altar, he continued in a tone of inspiration—

"Yes, even in this life, when the cross seems heaviest to be borne—when poverty, disease, and sin, have crushed man's spirit, even then our guardian angel bids us hope and pray! None who are children of the Church can complain that they are ever deserted by their affectionate mother. There is a fountain of mercy ever open in the sacred tribunal of Penance. In the most blessed sacrament of the Altar, lo! as He promised, Jesus ever dwells amongst us; and in the Holy Communion truly we feed upon the bread of life. Death itself is shorn of his terrors; even along his cold and awful path, the soul is still upheld. Ministering spirits hover o'er it, bidding it welcome to a better life! And she, the Queen of Saints, Mary, the most Immaculate Mother of God, offers on its behalf the most tender prayers for mercy to her Saviour and her Son."

Pausing, as if overpowered by the glorious ideas thus presented to the seeker after truth, and slowly raising his eyes and hands towards heaven, the bishop bade God's blessing rest upon his flock, in the name of Father, Son, and Holy Ghost.

CHAPTER X.

"HERE we are, now, within three weeks of leaving town; the season will be over, and, after making every one believe it was your intention to propose to that sweet girl, Edith Paget, you have not yet done so. Really, Frank," said Lady Blanche Vavasour, you are enough to provoke a saint! The *belle* of the season, and almost the richest heiress in London!—why, one would think you must be mad to risk by any delay the chance of securing such a prize. And how a man involved as you are can be so blind to his own interests astonishes me; for if you imagine your father either will or can assist you, I tell you plainly there is no hope from that quarter. Only the other day he told me he feared you would have to sell out, as he could not continue to make you so large an allowance."

"My dear mother," replied the handsome exquisite, "*vraiment*, you have astonished even me. I had no idea the family affairs were in the shaky state you hint at. As to my own, I have long been aware of their desperate condition; and, but for fear of injuring our corps, my creditors would have made a stir long since. *Hélas!* they are moving now. Look," he continued, taking a letter from his pocket-book, "at this notice I received from that Jacques this morning—his bill is over five hundred; and he vows if I don't send him a cheque this week he will sue me! So, you see, mother mine, the necessity for the sale you mentioned has arrived. The sons of Abraham are deaf to all my little requests for accommodation."

"Most assuredly, unless you consent to marry,"

replied Lady Blanche, "there is no other path open to you. But once let your creditors hear that your engagement with Edith Paget is a settled affair, and, from clamorous duns they will at once become your most obedient and humble servants. We shall meet her at Lady Grant's to-night, and depend upon me for securing you an opportunity for making the proposal." And, kissing him fondly, his mother quitted the room.

No one would have guessed that a fearful secret lay, like a leaden weight, on the heart of the handsome guardsman. If there was a shade of care upon that noble brow, it might have been attributed to pecuniary difficulties. And yet, no sooner had the door closed on him, than he sank into a chair, covered his face with his hands, and tears—yes, tears!—forced themselves through his fingers. The picture his mother had drawn brought the past to his recollection, and a vision of a fair girl, to whom, in a foreign land, he had been secretly united, and whom, in spite of his many faults, he had really loved. He thought of her deserted—left a stranger and friendless—in a great city like London, where her very beauty would make her more liable to receive insults.

He had offered her up as a sacrifice on the altar

of pride! Writhing under the pangs of a guilty conscience, he resolved to reveal his true position to his father. But at that moment the evil one reminded him of his debts, the loss of social position, the disgrace of a forced sale of his commission, and at the same time whispered in his ear the wealth and honour now within his grasp. The time graciously allowed him to choose between good and evil had passed. Frank hastily arose, with the determination to decide his fate with Edith Paget that very night.

CHAPTER XI.

THE late Sir Hugh Paget, father of the "great heiress," was one of those proud and eccentric characters occasionally to be met with in the neighbourhood of old country places. He had married late in life, and having lost his wife at the birth of Edith, his child became to the desolate old man the one idolized object of his affection.

Never fond of gaiety, he withdrew almost entirely from society, and seldom did a visitor cross the threshold of Branston Court, with the exception of his old and valued friend Sir Thomas Freeman, the possessor of the adjoining estate, who, after having acted as his "fag" at Eton, and "chum" at Oxford, ended by becoming his trusty adviser, and ever welcome companion.

A strange and touching sight was it to watch those two old men, seated in the ancient oak-panelled library at Branston Court, the many-tinted sunbeams streaming through the painted windows on the shining curls of little Edith, then a beautiful little girl five years old. She was seated lovingly on her father's knee, listening with childish delight to the wonderful history of "Puss in Boots," which she had coaxed him to relate.

It would be difficult to say which of those two old men loved their tiny companion the best.

A cripple from an early age, Sir Thomas had remained through life a bachelor, and having but one very near relation, a spinster sister, his affection was divided between the latter and his friends at Branston Court.

It was, then, with sincere pleasure that he had acceded to his friend Sir Hugh Paget's dying request that he would act as his daughter's guardian. It was some years previous to the commencement of our tale that Edith had removed to Somerton Priory, where, under the joint care of Sir Thomas and his sister, she had grown up into a lovely and accomplished girl.

Accustomed as she had been from babyhood to be the idol of her father, she found no diminution of affection as an inmate of Somerton Priory.

Thus had the happy days of her childhood glided away, and it was not till she had reached the first sweet dawn of womanhood that the unpleasant truth flashed across her guardian's mind that his lovely ward should have a better opportunity of seeing the great world than could be obtained at the solemn dinners and parties of the county families. Yes, it was high time that Edith should make her *début* in London; and as neither Sir Thomas nor his sister felt equal to the task of introducing the new star into the hemisphere of fashion, it was resolved that a cousin of the Freemans, the Hon. Lady Clinton, should be requested to lend her valuable services as *chaperone* during the memorable season of 1851.

A widow, and with no children of her own, the request had been readily acceded to; and not only had she taken Edith to be presented at her first drawing-room, but having, in addition, introduced her to the *élite* of London society, she was amply rewarded by hearing Miss Paget proclaimed as the "*belle*" of the season.

To the initiated, what magic is there not to be found in that title!—what scenes of enchantment does it not disclose to the fortunate possessor!

It was at one of Lady Vavasour's balls that Edith first met Frank Vavasour, and, to do him justice, it was more from the *naïve* freshness of her conversation and manner, than with any idea of admiring her as the "great heiress," that he had paid her any marked attention. At this period he had not quite forgotten his deserted, innocent wife.

As to Edith, accustomed as she had been from childhood to adulation, her *début* into an atmosphere of flattery did not in the least destroy her natural simplicity of character. The titles and elevated position of many of the gentlemen visitors at Lady Clinton's had no attraction for her unworldly mind; but, in the congenial spirit of Frank Vavasour's she fancied, poor child, that she had realized her *beau idéal!* Introduced to her at his own mother's house, and his visits sanctioned by Lady Clinton, it had never entered into her imagination that there could be any reasonable objection to her intimacy with Captain Vavasour.

Of Lady Blanche Vavasour and the "bishop" Edith stood in no little awe. But she soon became very fond of Marion; and when riding or walking with Frank and his sister, a happier trio could hardly have been met with. Alas! how would both these fair, innocent girls have turned away in shuddering horror,—the one from an idolized brother, the other from one who was daily becoming an object of intense interest to her young heart, had they known the true explanation of a peculiar reverie into which he would sometimes fall, and which the sister attributed to his embarrassed circumstances, and Edith fondly hoped might be occasioned by his anxiety to discover whether she returned his love!

CHAPTER XII.

The living of Eastbury, situated at no great distance from the county residence of the bishop of ——, was held by the Rev. Charles Horton, chaplain to his lordship. For some time it had been an understood thing that at some future day Marion Vavasour would become the wife of the rector of Eastbury.

He was an extremely clever man, possessed an independent fortune, and in the opinion of the world, a more desirable match could hardly have been found. Among the young ladies of the county there were certainly not a few who envied Marion the chance of becoming the wife of so amiable an individual. His religious opinions, too, were identical with those held by the "bishop." It might be that he gave them greater publicity. But then, his lordship acted, as he said, most wisely in not pressing the question too closely as to what those opinions really were. He had already permitted practices in his diocese at variance with the teachings of the establishment to which he had sworn obedience. What authority could be produced for allowing such proceedings? If the State Church could furnish no precedent, vain would it be to take refuge in the theory of the "Anglo-Catholics," viz., that they are but seeking to revive an order of things which a lax generation has suffered to fall into desuetude.

Still more futile would be the attempt to blind the Protestant people by the assertion that theirs "is a branch of the Catholic Church," and at the same time, disavow its connection with its parent trunk, viz., the Church of Rome!

Surely the idea is too absurd, that a small body of men should set themselves up as the real representatives of that spiritual power which pervades every part of Christendom; or that there is anything in their teaching which warrants the assertion that they are the legitimate successors of the apostles!

In calling themselves Catholics, they simply assume a name to which they have long forfeited all title. From whom do they hold their livings? Is it not confessedly from the state, whose glory would seem to be the constant boast of being essentially Protestant?

What is the result when a clergyman of the Church of England resigns his living from conscientious motives, and joins the Church of Rome? So long as he was satisfied to form a part of the system whose workings we are endeavouring to describe in these pages, he was considered as an efficient member. His great talents were the theme of universal admiration, his name was blazened forth by the organ of their party, as the great champion of "Anglo-Catholicity." Behold him, "when," to use the cant phrase, "he has gone over?" What a change! Can it be of the great leader they are speaking? Where are those transcendent abilities? What change has come over the recent "Anglo-Catholic," that he should merit such contemptuous treatment? Reader, do you wish to know? Then hear the plain truth: by that one bold act of an honest man and a sincere Christian he has proved to the entire world the utter falsity of the system he has left, and has furnished another living witness to the delusion of Protestantism!

No man was more fully alive to the persecution and obloquy that would be his inevitable lot were he to break from his party and take the final step, than Charles Horton. But, he often asked himself, why take such an extreme course? Where was the difficulty of his maintaining his present position with perfect freedom of opinion? Had not A and B and a score of others, all good and honourable men, believed and taught as he did, and yet remained in the Church?

It was unpleasant, certainly, to address that tiresome "Low-Church" party from the pulpit at Eastbury, and in conversation the next day, to be almost obliged to explain or retract the doctrines he had meant them to understand! Yes; all this was the occasion of much anxiety; but when Marion Vavasour was his wife, and he was Dean of ——, he would brave the opinion of "those silly Evangelicals," and, if so inclined, would introduce confession in private, and candles and flowers, and a cross, with its "moveable crucifix" on the altar.

He was rather doubtful as to what Marion might say to all this; but then, he had the bishop for his authority. He should tell her that the times required "progression," and the "system" "development," that unless he endeavoured to restore the ancient splendour of the church, it would be vain to expect persons to leave the Roman Communion for the cold worship of the Anglican faith. Yes; when she returned, he really must set to work in earnest. Poor child! amid all that London gaiety, she could have no time to think of such things. Well, perhaps so much the better. Once in the country, he could, by degrees, unfold his views to her, and she was so amiable that there was no fear of her going too far.

CHAPTER XIII.

The great world of London—fashion and her votaries—were just awakening from their slumbers, far off in the west of Modern Babylon; but, in Belgravia, carriages were driving rapidly to and fro.

In one of the best-appointed of these splendid equipages might be seen, hastily making his way to the House of Lords, Francis Vavasour, bishop of ——.

The night of the ——, 1851, was one likely to be remembered, not only by the state clergy, of which his lordship was so distinguished a member, but by the whole of England. The streets were thronged by groups of people, all manifesting the greatest anxiety to ascertain the intentions of Government with respect to the "Ecclesiastical Titles Bill," which was to come on for discussion that night.

There were not a few of the inhabitants of London who dreaded lest their Catholic fellow-citizens, remembering the many insults heaped upon their faith for many months, might choose that night to revenge themselves for the injustice of years!

Whilst crossing —— Street, the "bishop's" carriage was blocked up for a few moments by a line of cabs and other vehicles. On looking out to ascertain the cause, his glance fell upon a priest, who was waiting for an opportunity to cross the road. The "bishop" started uneasily, for his eyes had just met those of his only brother, Julian Vavasour.

Long years had passed since those brothers had met face to face, and a tide of recollections swept over the memory of Francis Vavasour, bringing vividly before him the bright days of their boyhood. A slight feeling of compunction also crossed his mind, as he looked at the pale face and wasted figure which contrasted so strongly with his own. Here was one of those very bishops against whom he was preparing to utter the most sweeping denunciations for having dared to assume a title in direct contravention to both human and divine law. But, to establish this point, he must go back to the very foundation of apostolic succession. He must talk much of the " primitive bishops " of the " ancient Church of the apostles," and make it clear that he, Francis, " bishop " of ——, formed a link in the chain of succession; whereas, men in the position of his brother and the so-called bishops were pretenders.

He took one glance more at his brother, as the carriage now began to move onwards, and, like a voice from the unseen world, came the thought to his mind, "Thou shalt not bear false witness against thy brother." There was a struggle in the heart of Francis Vavasour for a few moments, and its traces were visible upon his features as he took his seat in the House of Lords. Those who saw the marks of excitement on his face attributed them entirely to natural anxiety regarding the important subject upon which he was about to speak.

An orator from his youth,—possessed of that marvellous gift of language that enabled him so to clothe a discourse as to completely enchain the hearts of his audience, never had the "bishop" more forcibly appealed to the reason, the interests, the passions of that noble assembly than on the eventful night in question.

In words of thrilling power, he told the peers of England "that unless they voted as one man against the right of a foreign potentate to confer Ecclesiastical Titles within the realm of England, that neither the throne or altar would be secure from intrusion. That this was but the beginning of an end. That once concede that right, liberty itself would be but a name!"

In the midst of applause, such as is but seldom heard within those stately walls, a faint cry was suddenly heard, and he, who an instant before seemed the embodiment of physical and mental vigour, sank back in his seat a helpless victim to the dread foe paralysis.

Gently they bore the distinguished orator in his carriage to Belgrave-square. All the medical skill that London could supply was instantly assembled round his lorship's bed.

There was yet hope; for though the power of

speech seemed extinct, the mind of the sufferer remained untouched.

Little could any of those who tended that sick bed imagine the awful punishment it was to Francis Vavasour to hear the constant repetition of that voice, which but a few short hours since had given utterance to what he now felt was intended for a merciful warning.

CHAPTER XIV.

THE memorable ball given by Lady Grant has passed off triumphantly, and—thanks to Blanche Vavasour's skilful manœuvring — the great prize in the matrimonial market has been secured. Edith Paget, the "*belle* of the season," and the richest heiress of England, has become the affianced bride elect of Captain Vavasour.

The columns of the *Morning Post* have proclaimed the important fact to the world of fashion, the heart of Lady Blanche Vavasour throbs proudly, and her still lovely face is decked with its brightest smiles, as she listens to the oft-repeated congratulations of her vast circle of friends.

Yes; for this hour she had, indeed, long hoped, and even prayed! With pure, unselfish affection did she love her only son; and now her fondest desires are realized, and her idol would more than ever be worshipped by society and its votaries.

For once! even the tongue of envy could find nothing to utter against the "*belle* of the season." The simple, unpretending manners of Edith Paget had won all hearts, and there was almost a tone of tenderness in the expressed desire for her happiness uttered by the world in which she lived.

Shrinking almost from her own thoughts Edith half trembled at the idea that the heart which she had so much desired to win was actually her own! That a time was coming when the object of her first pure, warm affections would be all in all to her,—one to whom she must look up as well as love, reverence as well as obey. "No hard task that," whispered the young girl's heart. Already she regarded her affianced husband as a model of perfection, and her only fear, as she told Lady Clinton, when revealing her engagement, was that she had not deserved to look forward to a life of such perfect happiness!

Dream on, young heart! for only once in a woman's life comes there a vision of love,—real, unselfish, unworldly, true affection! — love, such as we can imagine the Great Father of us all intended should fill the heart of man, as well as woman, but a love that is seldom to be found in these degenerate days.

For, what is the fashionable idea of marriage? Rank, fortune (perhaps beauty), a splendid ceremony in the one church, that would seem to be dedicated rather to Hymen than St. George, followed by a long description of guests, dresses, and presents to the bride, given in the columns of the *Morning Post*.

The stream of life flows on as before, " Love's young dream" passes away like a vision of the night, and the young girl wakes to find that she has been made the victim to a *mariage de convenance*. The mask of society falls from the face of her husband, and the idol of her first affection stands revealed in his natural character!

Great was the excitement in the quiet household of Sir Thomas Freeman, when Captain Vavasour's letter, asking his consent to an engagement with his lovely ward, reached Somerton Priory. It was with smiles and tears that Edith's very long one was read, both by the baronet and his sister. The very retirement in which they lived made the idea even stranger to them, that one, whom they regarded as a "child," was actually engaged to enter upon the most solemn duties of a woman's life! That Edith would return only to leave them for ever in their old age for the care of a stranger, was a sad and painful thought both to Sir Thomas and Miss Freeman.

But "Edith's welfare was concerned," "Edith's feelings must alone be considered," and so, with a sigh for the past, Sir Thomas wrote a gracious acceptance of Captain Vavasour's proposal, while Miss Freeman sat down to write a long, loving letter to her darling, urgently begging her to return at once to Somerton Priory, and assuring her of a warm reception for Captain Vavasour, whenever he could find it convenient to pay them a visit.

CHAPTER XV.

Time has flown swiftly by since we took leave of Mrs. Tichborne in the humble dwelling in St. George's Fields. The object of her tender solicitude had amply repaid her care, and in the lovely being who bent gracefully over her harp, as she swept its chords with a master's hand, few would have recognized the poor suffering Violet, the recital of whose miseries had so touched the warm heart of Mrs. Tichborne in the sacristy of St. George's Cathedral.

Yes, it was indeed Violet, but changed; oh, how changed did she feel life had become for her! Days and weeks glided away, and found her only still more inclined to invoke rich blessings on the head of one who had proved to be not only a friend, but a most loving mother. Not a cloud was there to overshadow her perfect happiness, save the remembrance of her still idolized, though faithless husband. At thought of him the bitter tears would fall. Ah, well! child of a faith which teaches that trial and sorrow meet us at almost every step, from the cradle to the grave, one hope at least she had, one refuge ever open to her—she could pray! She had been united to her husband by the sacrament of matrimony. The graces attendant on its worthy reception would surely be hers, for she had entered on the holy state in the spirit of a Christian and a Catholic. Therefore she resolved to wait patiently and hopefully the issue of her prayers.

Never had Mrs. Tichborne, either by word or deed, given the least idea to Violet that her husband or his family were known to her. In this mode of action she was warmly seconded by the Abbé Jean, who had supplied her with the fullest information regarding the marriage.

The news of Francis Vavasour's engagement to Edith Paget somewhat hastened Mrs. Tichborne's plan. On reading the announcement in the *Morning Post*, she saw at once that no time was to be lost, if she intended to counteract the plot against poor Violet's happiness. Carefully removing the morning papers, she announced to Violet her intention of giving a grand concert, at which it was her express desire she should perform, and she should be introduced to the guests as Miss Acton, that having been Mrs. Tichborne's maiden name. The waning season had made long invitations unnecessary, so that at the expiration of a few days a brilliant throng of all the fashionables still in town were assembled in the splendid salons of Mrs. Tichborne, —— Street, Grosvenor Square.

"Beautiful," "exquisite," were the low murmurs that met Mrs. Tichborne's ear, as she led Violet to the harp. "A rival even to the *belle* of the season,' were it not almost treason to utter such a thing," said the old Duke of Bradley, as he drew near the charmed circle which was gathered round the beautiful harpist.

A suppressed "hush" was audible as, with a voice of exquisite sweetness, Violet commenced the "Incarnatus" of Pergolesi. The voice of the singer, as she uttered the soul-subduing words, rose higher and higher, so that the ears of the audience in the distant rooms could catch the notes. Striking a chord that at once vibrated in the hearts of all who stood in rapt attention around her, she paused; and at that instant raising her eyes towards heaven, they fell upon a group composed of Francis Vavasour, Edith Paget, Marion, and Lady Blanche Vavasour, who had just entered the room, and stood as if entranced by the tones of that exquisite voice!

The arm on which Edith Paget was leaning trembled so violently that she turned anxiously to her lover's face in order to ascertain the cause.

Greatly was she alarmed to perceive, that not only was that much-loved face of a ghastly pallor, but his features also wore an expression of terror for which she could in no way account.

Following the direction of his eyes, her own rested on the beautiful face of Violet "Acton," which exhibited evident traces of agitation. This was enough for the eye of affection; and poor Edith felt but too plainly that it told of a mystery in which she had never been a sharer.

Who that has ever experienced the intrusion of the first doubt regarding a beloved one, but must too well remember the bitter agony of that moment?

No word of inquiry escaped from Edith's lips. Young and gentle as she was, she possessed that woman's pride which could seal her lips, even though the heart that throbbed so wildly broke in the struggle.

Only uttering the words, "Tell Lady Blanche

I should like to find a seat," she suffered Francis Vavasour to conduct her to one, when he instantly quitted the room.

To rush into the conservatory, which was now deserted, to throw himself upon a couch and burying his head in its pillows, strive to shut out the past, the present, and the future, was the first action of the wretched young man.

Oh how he cursed the moment when he first swerved from the path of duty, and deserted his young and trusting wife!

Was it a shade from the tomb that he had just seen, come back to warn him to repent? or was it, as his heart too plainly told him, his beautiful Violet, snatched, as by a miracle, from the destitution and starvation in which he had so long left her?

The very air she sang was one he well remembered as having been her favourite. Often, in the early days of their married life, she had sung it for him, and tried to make him feel the solemn truths of its glorious words.

He pictured to himself his fair young wife surrounded by other men,—thought of the attentions her position as the beautiful "Miss Acton" would oblige her to receive,—and he almost groaned at the idea that he, who alone possessed the right to her affection, had, by his own folly, lost all claim to her slightest consideration. For, had he not outraged every feeling of affection, and added insult to injury, by publicly appearing before her as the affianced of another?

The evening had not been altogether free from anxiety for Lady Blanche Vavasour. Her watchful eye had noted her son's extreme agitation and abrupt disappearance. What if others had remarked it,—and what must his bride elect and Lady Clinton think at his prolonged absence?

Far, very far was Lady Blanche from guessing the real cause of her son's conduct. She had remarked Violet's extreme beauty, and knowing Mrs. Tichborne to have several nieces, whom, from the circumstance of their having been educated abroad, she had never seen, she imagined this might be "the" Miss Acton of whom she had heard her son speak. Knowing Sir James Acton to be a strict Catholic, she set down the mutual agitation of her son and "Miss Acton" to the fact of some boy-and-girl attachment which doubtless did not suit the views of the young lady's family.

But there was another source of annoyance in

store for Lady Blanche Vavasour upon this eventful evening.

On her first entrance into Mrs. Tichborne's drawing-room, her eye rested on the tall figure of her despised brother-in-law, Julian Vavasour. Yes; there he was, standing close behind Violet "Acton's" harp, his face more pale and careworn than usual, though the intelligent dark eyes had lost none of their lustre, as they rested with an expression of sadness, she fancied, on herself.

The man whom she had treated with so much scorn was actually in the same room, and she had the additional mortification of seeing Mrs. Tichborne take Marion up to Violet; and, after introducing the two young ladies, she perceived, with a feeling almost of rage, that the Bishop was engaged in earnest conversation with her daughter.

She was on the point of interrupting an interview she had long dreaded, when a murmur of voices reached her ears, and the words, "Sudden and dangerous illness of the 'Bishop' of ——" fell like an electric shock upon her troubled mind.

There was a scene of grief and confusion, and

in a few minutes the whole of that brilliant party which had accompanied Lady Blanche was on its way to the house of mourning in Belgrave Square.

CHAPTER XVI.

A MEMORABLE one the London season has proved to many a fair *débutante;*—an eventful one it has been to the promoters of the world's wonder—the Crystal Palace!

But what beneficial results will accrue to those "great unwashed"—the people? Dare we hope for a new order of things amongst a higher class of the population—our clever artisans and mechanics?

Will the mere sight of all those grand productions of man's hand teach such as these no higher lesson than to strive yet more earnestly to excel all other nations in scientific and mechanical improvements!

Could not some among the many beautiful

objects of ancient and modern art have first attracted the attention, and then whispered, as it were, to the heart of perhaps one earnest gazer in that court of a mediæval age,—

"We tell of a time when your merrie England honoured the one ancient Church, for whose glorious services we were made. Our place then in your vast city would have been upon the altar of your great cathedral. This exquisite monstrance, enriched with costly gems, would there, in its legitimate home, have contained that Sacred Presence which would have proved an object of adoration to thousands of devout worshippers."

If no such thoughts as these passed through the minds of the great bulk of visitors to that court, so rich in its associations to Catholics, there was at least one individual to whom the "chalice" and "monstrance," in their silent eloquence, appealed to the imagination and yet more forcibly to the heart. Day by day might Marion Vavasour be found gazing, as if lost in thought, on the case containing the sacred vessels; and various had been the surmises excited in the worldly mind of Lady Blanche, to account for her daughter's frequent and protracted visits to that court. "Could it be" (but the idea was too absurd) "that Marion was drifting towards Catholicism?"

Unknown to those among whom she lived, a strange change had indeed come over Marion. For some years past had she experienced intense yearnings after truth, and been conscious of a void in her soul's affections, which the religion of the best of those among whom she lived could never fill.

In visiting her favourite church, the venerable Westminster Abbey, she had often felt a sense of desolation that seemed to chill her feelings of devotion.

She could not forbear reverting to the period when, filled with devout worshippers, there had been a meaning, a reality, in the exquisite and solemn services of the ancient faith.

Some might indeed urge that the liturgy remained unchanged. Alas! those who employ such an argument would seem to be content with the possession of the casket, after the precious gem which alone made it valuable has been lost!

The prayers, though mutilated and distorted, are still used; but, the one great act of worship, the holy sacrifice of the Mass, is no longer as in the olden days, the great centre whence those beautiful prayers all radiate! Then, too, open were the massive doors of the cathedral to the artisan, who could, without the aid of beadle or guide, find his way to the altar of the most Holy Sacrament, and there implore a blessing on the labours of the day.

Kneeling before the shrine of England's regal Confessor, might be seen the rich and the poor, and no verger's voice grated harshly on the ears of the pious suppliants, "Rise! no praying to him is allowed!"

No! the church in those days was the home of the poor; who gladly exchanged their own miserable dwellings for such a glorious temple, where their souls were fortified with religious consolation, and their minds elevated by gazing on the beautiful productions of art.

One hears much in these days of the awful depravity of the great masses of the people, but the lamentable fact ceases to be an object of astonishment, when we reflect on the practical heathenism in which so many of them live.

The rich Puritan, who takes his six days' round of pleasure, be it either the religious dissipation of the Exeter Hall May Meetings, or the more worldly recreations of his "position," has little consideration for the overstrained minds and bodies of poor artisans and labourers. These, pent up during the long weary hours which compose their week, and inhaling a fetid atmosphere, are thankful enough, when the blessed Sunday comes to give them time and liberty to go forth, it may be, into the quiet country, and breathe the fresh air of heaven. Vain effort to attempt to dictate to such men, and, bidding them don their "sabbath suit," consent to sit for hours in "sad civility," listening to the pious twaddle of some Rev. Dryasdust! No; the reality of religion, all that could bring it home to the imagination and hearts of the people, is carefully excluded. They are forbidden to gaze on holy pictures; and to look with eyes of veneration on the image of the Crucified, they are taught to regard as a "deadly sin."

CHAPTER XVII.

It was with a feeling of deep sorrow at her young heart, that Edith Paget, on reaching home in Eaton Place, after suffering her maid to prepare her toilet for the night, seated herself in her luxurious dressing-room, and, resting her beautiful head upon her small white hand, sank into a reverie of painful meditation.

Her glance rested for a moment on the sparkling diamond hoop upon her slender finger, and a bitter sigh escaped her as she gazed. It was the pledge of her betrothment to Francis Vavasour!

A presentiment of coming evil fell like the dark shadow of the approaching storm upon her already over-excited mind, and tears, which it was almost agony to shed, flowed down her pale face. And thus did poor Edith "outwatch the slow-paced night," a prey to the most intense mental suffering which it falls to the lot of woman to endure. She felt that she had given her fresh, unworldly love to one who, if he did love her in return, it could not be with the same affection which she felt for him. Or why (painful and bitter thought) had he shown such marked agitation at the sight of another?

Strange and inexplicable power which woman possesses of reading the heart of the man she loves! It was from this mysterious knowledge Edith felt that the tie between herself and Francis Vavasour was for ever broken.

She would take no hasty steps; oh, no! her heart even now whispered that he had nothing to dread from her. Besides, was he not in sorrow?

There was Marion, too, that beloved friend whom it had been one of her fondest hopes to call by the still more endearing name of sister! She thought of the many hours of pleasant converse passed together; and the remembrance of the pure and holy lessons of simple faith in the mercy of eternal love which Marion, by precept and practice, had striven to teach her, fell like precious balm upon her wounded spirit. Rising from her chair, she sank upon her knees, and from her grief-laden heart there breathed forth to the ear of Omnipotence, ever open to His erring children's cry for help, "'Father! not my will, but thine be done.' Send me peace, but not of this world!"

And peace came softly, like the fanning of an angel's wing. And hope, the messenger of glad tidings, pointed to heaven, and that blessed time when tears and sorrow should be unknown!

CHAPTER XVIII.

SITUATED at no great distance from Branston was a pile of ecclesiastical-looking buildings, which were a constant source of annoyance to the pious Miss Stellard and her "Society for the Extinction of Roman Catholics." Great had been the amount of energy displayed by the worthy members, to prevent the Papists from securing a spot of ground whereon to erect what the organ of their party, the *Branston Firebrand,* stigmatised as the "House of Mystery."

In vain, however, was a public meeting held, at which awful revelations had been made by a great champion of Protestantism, touching "the horrors daily committed in the convents of Italy," and of which he professed to have been a witness!

Idly did these sayings and doings fall upon the ear of one of the most wonderful women of our day, and whom God, in special mercy, seems to have raised up in order to teach those ignorant of Christian doctrine the truths of Scripture as interpreted by the one infallible Church.

When has it ever been known that "Mother Margaret" failed in even one of her great undertakings to found convents for the extension of her Order?

Regardless of the storm of Protestant abuse, she laboured on, and her efforts were rewarded by seeing her beautiful convent completed, and filled with those pious "sisters" whose daily lives are one continued act of faith and love.

Despite the efforts of Miss Stellard and her clique to poison the minds of the Branston poor, it was impossible for those who had been tended with so much care by these maligned Catholic ladies to believe that they who had watched by the deathbed of a husband or child stricken down by fever, could be the monsters of iniquity they were represented.

No; for once faith and charity triumphed over

malice and bigotry, and many a poor man and woman blessed God for sending beneath their humble roof those "angels of mercy."

Any one less sanguine than Mother Margaret might well have been dismayed, not alone at the bigotry, but the awful amount of heathenism she found herself thrown amongst. It was no uncommon occurrence for her and her sisters, when conversing with the poorer classes, to discover that they were ignorant of even the name of the Saviour. Many were leading a mere animal existence, without a thought or desire beyond the present life; dragging on their wretched lives, devoid even of one external object that might call into action the dormant faculties of their immortal souls.

And yet such is the perversity of human nature, it is against the efforts of such holy instruments as Mother Margaret and her nuns to work out the regeneration of her degraded sons and daughters, that England, in almost every pulpit, platform, book, and newspaper, is waging so dishonourable, so unholy a warfare. What if we concede that never before was there a period when so much was done to educate the people? Is it not a most indisputable fact that, in spite of the schoolmaster being abroad, there is an amount of crime in the towns and villages of England, that the highest dignitaries of the Established Church have confessed themselves unequal to cope with?

The boasted watchwords, "Liberty, Equality, Fraternity," would appear to develope themselves in England into liberty of practical infidelity, fraternity of rationalism, and equality of scepticism.

It has been reserved for the nineteenth century to proclaim to the Christian world that it is quite possible for men, believing and teaching rank Socinianism, some doubting baptismal regeneration, others even denying the atonement of Christ, while a minority proclaims its strict adherence to Catholic doctrines, to unite together into a body, having, it now appears, for an infallible authority, not the Word of God, but the Thirty-nine Articles.

When will teachers and rulers of England comprehend that a time is fast coming when education itself will cause the lower orders to ask why it is that their " Established Church " is so rent and torn by intestine divisions. Yes; a study of history will teach even such as these that there was a time when the Catholic religion embraced within her ample pale the length and breadth of England; that in those ages of faith, poverty was not a crime; that if the ancient Church possessed immense revenues, they were always considered as the heritage of Christ's poor; that it was a Protestant king who alienated from the monks and nuns the property which those servants of religion held in trust for the poor of England; that to a Protestant queen are the poor indebted for that godless refuge of the destitute—the workhouse; and this in exchange for the hospitable convents and monasteries, with their free schools for the children of the poor, and free hospitals, whose doors were ever open to succour and relieve all who needed advice or assistance.

CHAPTER XIX.

The bright rays of a midday sun were streaming through the latticed windows of the convent of "Our Lady of Mercy." The fine old trees in the spacious garden offered a tempting shade to any one disposed, on that lovely summer's day, for solitude and meditation.

The drowsy hum of the honey-seeking bee, the soft chime of "Angelus" falling sweetly on the ear, and reminding even the sons of toil to pause for a moment, and raise their thoughts from earth to heaven; the quiet figures of the pious nuns proceeding forth on their daily errands of charity, formed a picture of such perfect happiness, as might well cause the heart of Violet Vavasour to throb with an unusual and deeper sense of God's mercy.

Had it been possible for Violet entirely to forget the bitter past, she might perchance have found the jewel of contentment amid scenes like these. But too well had she loved her faithless husband ever to forget him. The sight of him had recalled the days of their early married life, when she certainly possessed his affection.

Alas! it was with a bitter pang at her heart she pictured to herself the great change that must have come over him ere he could have so far forgotten his duties as her husband as actually to engage himself to another.

The only earthly drop of comfort in her cup of sorrow was the agitation he had shown when his glance met hers at Mrs. Tichborne's concert. The look of amazement with which he for an instant regarded her, had in a moment given place to one of deep tenderness; and assured did Violet feel that, save from a dread of an exposure before Mrs. Tichborne's guests, he would at once have cast himself at her feet.

It was with a feeling of intense pleasure she had acceded to the express wish of Mrs. Tichborne and Father Julian, that she should make a retreat, under the care of Mother Margaret, in the beautiful convent near Branston. Not only would she enjoy there more fully than in town the holy consolations of her much-loved faith, but she would have—and this of itself constitutes one great charm of a visit to a convent—the daily pleasure of seeing and conversing with one or another of the religious.

Oh, if those who utter such cowardly calumnies against the nuns could experience the peace, the holiness, the purity, that seem to pervade the very atmosphere of the cloister, and the sense of holy repose which fills the soul as we listen to their pious conversation! If they could behold the daily lives of these heroic women; see them treading so meekly in the footsteps of their great

Master, whose path was ever the narrow way of the Cross, would not the blush of shame crimson their cheeks on discovering that a blow had been given to Christ himself in the persons of his humble followers?

CHAPTER XX.

BANKSIDE, the country residence of the Bishop of ——, was situated in one of the most picturesque portions of the county of ——. Half hidden in its park-like grounds, it was the favourite abode of the family—a fact made evident by the care taken with the exquisite gardens, and the air of nameless elegance which a refined taste never fails to impart to the home of its affections. A slight improvement in the "bishop's" health had enabled him to remove to Bankside; and now, apparently, all seemed to the worldly heart of Lady Blanche to be progressing in accordance with her wishes.

Frank, the dearest object of her affections, was actually engaged to Edith Paget; and to unite

Marion with Charles Horton should, so she resolved, be the result of their country recess.

It was a lovely evening in August, and Marion, who had been to visit some poor pensioners, was slowly driving her pony-chair up the hill past the church, when the gate leading from the vicarage garden was flung back, and the Rev. Charles Horton made his appearance.

He was looking very grave, for he had that day attended a tiresome vestry meeting, where an obstinate churchwarden belonging to the Low-Church party had annoyed him by asking whether the report that he was " going over to Rome," which appeared in the *Branston Firebrand*, was correct? Called upon thus publicly to avow his real opinions, or at once to deny his most cherished " Anglo-Catholic " convictions, had proved a most bitter ordeal. Much, very much, of what he really did believe, he had endeavoured to explain away; but, guarded as his language had been, the impression fixed itself on his mind as he was quitting the vestry, that though not daring to say so openly, few of those who had listened to his explanation believed him to be speaking the entire truth.

A smile of pleasure passed over his pale face as

he returned Marion's greeting, and accepted her invitation to return with her to Bankside.

"And now, Mr. Horton," said Marion, "having told you all about my gaieties, I am anxious to have some serious conversation with you."

An ashy paleness spread over the face of the worthy clergyman on hearing these, to him, ominous words, and it was with a desperate struggle he so far overcame his emotion as to reply, with but a melancholy attempt at a laugh,—

"Indeed, lady fair! What can you have to ask me that causes you to look so grave?"

"It is a subject that is puzzling wiser heads than mine — I mean about this strife in the Church. Each day is it becoming more and more difficult for such as I am to understand what it is we are to believe. And if to us, who have so many opportunities of learning the truth, it be so hard to discover which party in the Church is the right one, what are the ignorant poor to do? how are they to decide? And, when we see how crime is multiplying in our land, and faith itself becoming each day, save to the chosen few, a thing of the past, oh, how every soul that really loves its God must mourn over the divisions that are amongst us, and humbly pray for the return of the 'one faith, one Lord, one baptism!'—the faith which realizes the saving truths of religion—the faith which, through the graces of its most blessed, life-giving sacraments, makes us, even in this life, feel that we are near, so very near, to immortality. And this faith, which can alone restore to our land the noblest title which she ever bore—I mean that of 'Catholic England,'—is the 'milk-white hind' which the ministers of your State Church continue to pursue with unrelenting hatred."

"You amaze me, Marion!" were the first words uttered by Mr. Horton. "Am I to understand that you actually wish to re-establish the 'Roman' Catholic as the dominant religion? Surely, you can find enough in the Anglo-Catholic faith to satisfy the devotional cravings of the most earnest soul! And each day we are endeavouring more and more to revive the ancient order of things. True, indeed, we cannot yet venture to do all that we hope to effect in course of time; for we have fearful opposition to contend against, especially from the bigoted, ultra-low-church party. But, considering the great progress we have made, there is very much to encourage us to hope for the future. I must take your enlightenment into my hands, make you out a list of the books I wish you to read; and, if you like it, you shall make your first confession to me."

"The question which I cannot make any of you 'Anglo-Catholics' answer," said Marian, "is, by what authority you teach the things which you do? You belong to a Protestant Church, and you preach doctrines which she ignores! You talk of obedience, and refuse to show it to your superiors in that Church, when their views differ from those of your party! You have just named one doctrine, partly, I am aware, in jest—I mean Confession. By what means can I satisfy my own mind that, after having confessed to a Protestant clergyman, he has power to give the absolution? He has broken away from the golden chain of apostolic succession; he has separated himself from that Church whence bishops themselves derive all their authority. But, even allowing the supposition that he is rightly ordained, and has the *power* to give absolution, he can no more pardon sins without *jurisdiction*, than a Catholic priest can under similar circumstances. Besides, how can you believe yourselves the ministers of such a marvellous life-giving power, and at the same time teach the people that there are but 'two sacraments' in the Church?"

"If these are your real opinions, Marion," replied Mr. Horton, "it will be vain for me to reason with you. And yet I must endeavour to convince you that the authority of the 'Anglo-Catholic Church' is not so powerless as you seem to imagine. The great obstacle against which we have to contend at present is, the insane bigotry of the Low Church, opposed as it is to Convocation. Whilst the Church is united in unholy alliance to the State, it is vain to look for freedom of action. To what purpose revive or promulgate a doctrine which the verdict of a lay tribunal can set aside, or leave it an 'open question?' But, spite of this sad state of things, dear Marion, you should, like a 'true daughter,' be satisfied to remain within the bosom of your 'Mother Church,' hoping and praying for the glorious time when she will have shaken off the yoke which paralyses her energies, and, like a bride, come forth in all her splendour. Whilst thus waiting, her children, her true sons and daughters, may derive much comfort from the practice, if only in private, of those religious duties which, if properly understood, have power to impart much consolation to the soul."

"Then, if I understand you rightly, Mr. Horton," was Marion's somewhat indignant reply, "you admit that, according to law, you have no authority for what you teach. And we know that the Archbishop of Canterbury, the highest ecclesiastical authority in your Church, is equally opposed to you. Thus it is evident that you are simply carrying out the opinions of a small minority. For myself, I cannot but mourn deeply when I think of the awful spiritual peril of so many of my countrymen, who, in grasping at the shadow, are losing the substance, by contenting themselves with the mere ceremonial portion of the ancient Church.

"But," she continued, "a time of trouble, such as the world has never yet known, is rapidly approaching. The stormy waters of Rationalism, Socialism, Pantheism, and Infidelity, are swelling into a mighty torrent, that will soon burst the feeble barriers erected by the enthusiasm of the few. In that awful day, when this modern deluge of unbelief shall engulf multitudes of immortal souls, the 'ship of Peter,' like its antitype the ark, will ride triumphant over the stormy waves, because to her alone was that divine promise given, 'The gates of hell shall never prevail against you.'"

Anger, astonishment, and profound grief, in turns, filled Mr. Horton's mind, as he listened to Marion's open profession of the Catholic faith. That a "girl," a mere "child," should presume to set up her opinion in opposition to his, was a thing he could hardly believe. But, that this girl should have found time, during her first London season, to form such decided views of the Protestant Church, and the "Anglo-Catholic" portion of it in particular, deprived him almost of the power of reply.

However, as he gazed upon that exquisite, intellectual face, a softer feeling of deep sadness came over him. He thought of the gulf that now lay between them, as he heard from Marion's own lips an impatient declaration "that she could never be his wife." It seemed that the object of his existence was lost to him, and that he must plunge yet deeper into the strife of controversy, and thus seek to forget a time when he had dreamed of mutual love between himself and Marion Vavasour.

"And here, then, we part," said Marion, as

they came in sight of Bankside. "Think of me in your prayers, and I will pray that you may yet be brought into the Church of Christ."

A silent shake of the hand, a bow, and Charles Horton retraced his steps to the rectory, a sadder and a wiser man.

Marion re-entered Bankside with a feeling of depression, though rejoiced that the long-dreaded interview was over.

She could not help sympathizing with Mr. Horton, as she well knew what a shock the exposition of her religious opinions would be to him, and how he would grieve at losing the hope of her being his wife.

But she must either resign this human affection or her holy faith, and she had made her choice. Many a fervent petition had she sent up to Heaven that she might never swerve from her resolution.

Yes, her friends might look coldly upon her, and trials and sorrows might be her future portion; but the victory was won, and she blessed the mercy of God in permitting her to stand thus firmly, even in the porch of the "household of faith."

CHAPTER XXI.

We must now direct the attention of our readers to the movements of Captain Vavasour, whose absence from Eaton Place had been the subject of frequent conversation.

Busy tongues had already whispered at the clubs, and other fashionable haunts, that, after all, the "great heiress" might never enter the Vavasour family.

In the mean time, the unfortunate young man lay in the delirium of brain fever! The unexpected encounter with his wife at Mrs. Tichborne's eventful concert, and the pressure of his pecuniary affairs, had been the cause of his obtaining leave of absence from his regiment. In the gaieties of Paris he strove to forget for awhile his cares and troubles.

He had been but a short time in that brilliant capital ere he was attacked by fever, and for some weeks he continued a helpless victim to that terrible disease.

But, stranger as he was, charity had found and

ministered to him. The good people with whom he lodged had not only called in the first medical skill in Paris, but summoned to their aid the good Sisters of Charity, who attended the alien to their faith and country with the most tender devotion, and complete disregard of danger to themselves.

Were it not that each one's experience supplies proof that the drama of real life exhibits more extraordinary incidents than the most inventive writer of fiction can imagine, it might startle our readers to be told that, at the very time Captain Vavasour was in Paris, "Père Jean," who had married him only three years previously, was also there, and an inmate of the same house with the poor invalid!

But not one single event of our lives escapes the watchful eye of our Heavenly Father; and what a consolation it is to know that all which works for our good is the result of his providential care!

Slowly recovering from his severe illness, and a mere shadow of what he once had been, Captain Vavasour found himself able to bear removal to his sitting-room, and receive a visit from Père Jean.

There were traces of strong emotion on the face of the kind priest as he advanced to meet the invalid. For he had been a daily witness to the agony of the deserted wife, who, hastily summoned to what she feared might prove the deathbed of her husband, had, accompanied by Mrs. Tichborne, journeyed to Paris as rapidly as steamer and express could convey them.

Fearful of the shock a sudden interview with his wife might produce on the weakened nerves of Captain Vavasour, the physicians had decided that the Père Jean should first see the invalid, and, gradually leading him on to talk of past times, break to him the intelligence that Violet was even then under the same roof with him.

Severe illness had worked a salutary effect on the mind of Captain Vavasour. He had been brought face to face, as it were, with the "King of Terrors," and the remembrance of his narrow escape brought the tears of gratitude into his eyes.

It was with softened feelings such as these that he received the venerable Père Jean. The good priest's watchful care of him, together with that of the Sisters of Charity, had all been faithfully related to him. The prejudices that had been instilled into his mind against Catholic priests had faded away for ever before the bright light of charity.

It was a new and strange sensation to Captain Vavasour to find himself alone in Paris, listening with rapt attention to the pious conversation of a Catholic priest!

By God's grace, he had at length found the solution of that important problem, "What is truth?" Often before, in occasional pauses of the world's warfare, had he vainly endeavoured to solve it. For, to every human being there come at times moments of interior sadness; and, though all around seem bright, we feel that an immortal soul needs immortal love to satisfy its aspirations.

Kindly, and skilfully, did Père Jean lead Captain Vavasour to talk of those interior feelings which had, though silently, been working such a blessed change in the mind and heart of him who had hitherto been a mental infidel—a Christian in name only.

"And so, father," he continued, "while I watched at Oxford the workings of a great religious system, and the lives of those who were supposed to be preparing themselves to be spiritual guides to the people of England, I observed that, generally speaking, there was little to choose between their conduct and that of mere secular students. In after-life, I ceased to wonder at the contempt expressed for a system that can tolerate such a state of things. Indeed, can it be reasonably expected that men acquainted with the training of our state clergy should consult, or repose confidence in them? No; they have made up their minds that persons like these cannot minister to the diseases of the soul.

"Often, at my father's table, have I listened to the opinions of the clergy of all parties in the establishment upon the most important Christian doctrines, in the vain hope of discovering the truth. But there was no unity amongst them; and thus, to doubt succeeded still greater uncertainty. It seemed to me that I was at liberty to believe or reject, according to my private judgment. There was no other guide admitted. A small minority, indeed, professed to regard the Church as an authority, but could offer me no satisfactory reasons for trusting myself to her guidance. That some infallible authority did exist was a truth that gained upon me every day, and I experienced an irresistible attraction towards the centre of faith. When in conversation with my sister, I perceived the silent progress she had made in the knowledge of Catholicity, and the influence of religion on her daily life; I began also to wish to know something of a realized faith. I have told you, father, how deeply I sinned in forsaking my innocent wife, and the mental torture I afterwards endured. If aught could plead palliation for so foul a crime, it might be found in the dread I entertained of social persecution. Well I knew, that had I once acknowledged to my friends that I had so far outraged Protestant opinion as to marry a Catholic they would either shun my society or look coldly on me ever afterwards. England boasts that all her children enjoy liberty of conscience. But let this vaunted liberty be put to the test by either layman or clergyman publicly embracing the Catholic faith, and see what an outcry will be raised, what a system of social persecution will be brought to bear upon him! Only those who have been brought, by God's mercy, to see the folly of living slaves to the world's opinion, possess the courage to face it boldly. Yes, father, too well I know that I have sinned; but I have prayed for faith, and I feel that my life has been spared to enable me to perform a sacred work—that of redeeming the past."

When Captain Vavasour had concluded his narrative, Père Jean rose from his seat, and whispering a few words to his humble penitent, entered an adjoining room, where poor Violet had been anxiously waiting the result of the interview. He quickly returned, gently supporting his trembling companion. Placing her hand in that of her husband's, whilst tears of joy filled his eyes, he invoked a blessing on this happy union of soul as well as body, and hastily quitted the apartment.

We will follow his example, and draw a veil over that sacred scene where two human hearts, bound by a tie which death alone has power to sever, find themselves once again united.

CHAPTER XXII.

The anxious hearts of Sir Thomas and Miss Freeman had silently caused them to notice with deep sorrow the startling change in the appearance of their lovely ward, Edith Paget, when some two or three months afterwards she once more returned to their affectionate guardianship at Somerton Priory. A day or two after her arrival she had held a long interview with both those dearly loved friends.

Whatever the private thoughts and feelings of Sir Thomas and his sister might have been on the subject of their long discussion, both agreed that no further reference to it should ever again be made in the presence of their darling Edith.

So time passed on, but not without revealing to the watchful eye of affection the ravages of secret sorrow. Yes; Edith was indeed changed. The bright smile that was wont to light up her beautiful face, as with the golden touch of a sunbeam, had given place to that subdued *spi-*

rituelle expression, so symptomatic of interior blight.

Gazing upon her, as she was sitting in the fading light of an autumn evening in the bay window of the drawing-room at Branston Court, bitterly did Sir Thomas reproach himself for having suffered her to mix in the world, which had so soon exhibited itself to her as nothing but vanity and vexation of spirit. To shield Edith from even one mental or bodily pain, her kind old guardian would have spared no personal sacrifice. Hence, when, on her return to Somerton Priory, she had expressed a desire to spend some time at her old home at Branston Court, Sir Thomas and Miss Freeman at once consented without a murmur to bear her company.

Never did one complaint escape the lips of Edith Paget, as day by day she felt herself getting weaker. For some time past a presentiment had taken possession of her mind that her life would not be a long one. It gave her no pain, though she naturally experienced at intervals a feeling of sadness at the thought of leaving friends who loved her so fondly. But religion whispered to her, that a time would finally arrive when they would be all reunited in that "better land," whose light, though distant, is visible to the eye of faith.

Brought up from her youth in an atmosphere of sincere piety, Edith had ever been religiously disposed. Her first drive, on returning to Branston Court, had been to the daily service at Eastbury.

It was with no small pleasure that the rector, Charles Horton, observed the rich heiress take her place in his church; for he looked upon her as an instrument to bring about what he called Marion's reconversion.

Spite of the "dim religious light," which the stained windows cast over the "sanctuary," as Mr. Horton loved to call it, the altar with its unlighted candles and moveable cross, Edith never failed to experience a chill during her devotions each time she entered the church of Eastbury. There was, indeed, much to attract the eye in the artistic skill exhibited in its interior restoration. But Edith felt in her inmost soul, that a church thus restored most powerfully illustrated the obvious fact that the modern services therein performed bear a very slight resemblance to the ancient worship for which it was originally built.

Often and deeply did Edith ponder over these ideas, as, day after day she returned from the service at Eastbury. Yet, even as her earthly strength seemed to fail, came a low, soft whisper, as from an angel's voice, "Watch and hope: the dawn is near."

That all was at an end in this world between herself and Captain Vavasour, Edith well knew. But the news of his previous marriage had been a severe shock to her sensitive heart; and this was enough, in the opinion of her medical attendant, to develop the seeds of a disease which she had inherited from her young mother, as a dying legacy. The old family physician had gravely shaken his head, when hastily summoned to Branston Court, and had assured his anxious listeners "that Miss Paget's case was a question of time only."

Poor Sir Thomas Freeman, sinking into a chair, and bowing his grey head upon his shaking hands, gave full vent to the violence of his grief.

Yet, Edith heard without regret the sentence of her doom. For, to have loved, as woman loves but once in her life, with the pure disinterested love of a first affection, and then be rudely awakened to find it a painful dream, was indeed a bitter sorrow to endure. But even to those who patiently take up a heavy cross, is heavenly strength vouchsafed to bear its weight.

Poor Edith, sitting in the library at Branston Court, and poring over the tender letters she received from Marion Vavasour, began to feel the light of faith breaking on her soul.

CHAPTER XXIII.

PAINFULLY as Marion had been shocked by the extraordinary revelation regarding her brother's marriage, and the news of his alarming illness, she felt, whilst sharing the duties of the sick-room with his faithful wife, that from herself alone should now come those consolatory letters which she well knew the affectionate heart of poor Edith would so greatly prize.

It was a great comfort to Marion's somewhat overtaxed spirit to find in Violet a more than sister—one who could enter into the most sacred feelings of her heart. They were indeed united by that holy bond, a common faith, which links soul to soul, and which is understood by the children of the one true Church alone.

To be in Paris with all its glorious associations of Catholic times, past and present, to kneel before the altar of Notre Dame, and feel the blessed truth that she was no longer an outcast from the one faith, was indeed a happiness to Marion.

Again, to be able to watch each day the religious life of Paris, pursuing its angelic mission of holiness and charity, and no longer entertain, as formerly, the absurd Protestant notion, that fashion and gaiety are alone the objects of worship to the inhabitants of the French metropolis.

No; Marion well knew, from personal observation, that, even in the most fashionable *quartiers* of Paris, are there to be found ladies of the highest rank who do not shrink from associating themselves with the different religious Orders in the performance of their various duties of charity.

Nor is their pity to be considered as wanting in sincerity should it sometimes happen that the delicate hands which in the morning may have tended the deathbed of some moral leper of their own sex, are seen in the evening glittering with sparkling gems. It is not required that the duties of charity should monopolize all our time and attention.

Happy those who belong to that one Catholic faith which inculcates on the rich and highborn the duty of "doing good"—a duty nowhere so well observed as in the inner life of Parisian society.

It was not surprising that Marion found it an easy task to write the interesting letters which she did to Edith Paget.

There was so much to describe, not merely the well-known attractions of Paris, so much as the new, strange feelings which filled her own heart. Looking back, Marion sometimes fancied herself under the influence of a dream, living as she did at present with her brother and his wife, and that dear valued friend, Mrs. Tichborne, attending daily services at the Catholic church, visiting convents, conversing with priests and bishops, and, greatest happiness of all, receiving instruction from the celebrated Père de Ravignan, prior to her speedy admission into the Church. Truly she had enough to fill her thoughts and supply matter for letters. Often Mrs. Tichborne's anxious gaze would fix upon her, and many a fervent prayer would she breathe that the grace of perseverance might be hers.

When at length the long-desired day arrived, and Marion read her profession of faith in the exquisite chapel of the convent of the Sacré Cœur, the feelings of those two hearts were too big for utterance. As Mrs. Tichborne clasped Marion in a warm embrace, no interchange of language was required between them in order to make them feel that a link of love was now formed, binding them together in the golden chain of a common faith.

CHAPTER XXIV.

WORDS could not describe the anger of Lady Blanche when the news of Marion's having joined the Church of Rome reached her at Bankside.

It was not so much from the circumstance that a child of hers had dared to leave the established religion, of which the Bishop of —— was so distinguished a member, as the blow which her pride and bigotry had sustained.

The intelligence that her son had married a Catholic had been a severe shock. But she was able to console herself with the reflection that the lady being an "old Catholic," and a *protégée* of one who ranked as highly in society as did Mrs. Tichborne, her *monde* would easily forgive their former idol, Captain Vavasour, for marrying a beautiful and accomplished "Papist."

But as for Marion, the fatal step she had just taken had destroyed her prospects for life. Poor Lady Blanche almost groaned aloud, as, sinking into a *fauteuil*, she thought of the tones of affected condolence on her daughter's defection in which her noble friends would hasten to address her. It was the state of the bishop's health only which prevented her from starting off at once to Paris, in order to reason Marion out of her folly.

"Why not," sighed Lady Blanche, "rest content as an 'Anglo-Catholic,' with having mounted the first round of Peter's ladder, without ascending to its very summit? The 'Anglo-Catholic' in these days is the fashionable form of religion. Her dear friend the Duchess of Grantley had assured her that to be the *ton*, it was as essential to be seen at St. Margaret's as it was in her young days to be introduced at Almack's. There were to be found candles, crosses, exquisite music, and for those who aspired to such perfection, a private confessional (so the dear duchess had told her in a moment of confidence); why, then, should Marion rush blindly into a faith which the same distinguished authority whispered to her would never again be fashionable."

She finally concluded to send for Mr. Horton, who would advise her for the best under these annoying circumstances.

It was with a very grave face that Mr. Horton entered the drawing-room at Bankside.

As Lady Blanche, in a somewhat excited manner, detailed the account of Marion's having "gone over to Rome," he concealed all traces of emotion at the intelligence. But for a moment his affected composure was nearly overpowered, as his conscience upbraided him for his want of honesty in not following the dictates of what he too well knew was his own soul's conviction.

Lady Blanche was, it must be confessed, not a little surprised and scandalized at the quiet way in which the news of Marion's defection was received by Mr. Horton. Her astonishment did not diminish when he informed her "that it was no surprise to him to hear of it, and that he had noticed with pain the change in Marion's religious opinions on her return from London.

"It is very odd," replied Lady Blanche, "that her mother had seen nothing of the change he spoke of. To be sure, Marion would always go looking at those Catholic things in the Crystal Palace. But what would society think of a mere child like Marion taking a step so likely to produce an unpleasant notoriety? Those tiresome people, the Branston public, would soon hear all about it, and the entire family be held up to ridicule and insult in that odious paper, the *Branston Firebrand*."

Hastily rising from her chair, Lady Blanche led Mr. Horton to the door of the bishop's library, and left him to enter, whilst she proceeded to write an account of her troubles to the Earl of Burtonfell.

CHAPTER XXV.

Francis Vavasour, Lord Bishop of ——, was indeed sadly changed since the eventful night of that celebrated debate, when the "hand of God had touched him."

To the astonishment of the first physicians in London, he had recovered the use of his speech, and partially that of his limbs; but he looked considerably aged, and there was a subdued expression in his intellectual face very much at variance with the one it had formerly worn. Traces of an intense mental conflict were visible, from which, however, it was impossible for human ken to determine whether his good or evil genius had come off victorious.

For long months his lordship had sustained a powerful interior struggle, and the words, "Thou shalt not bear false witness against thy brother," had rung unceasingly in his ears. He began to feel and acknowledge to his own heart that the testimony he had borne against those Catholic bishops, of whom his brother Julian was one, was indeed false; for had it not been, as he now remembered with horror, his own constant endeavour, as an "Anglo-Catholic bishop," to prove his succession from those very men and that identical hierarchy which the wisdom of Pio Nono had judged fit to re-establish in England? As a sincere " Anglo-Catholic," had he for a moment believed that any of the links in the long chain of succession, from St. Peter to the present time, had been broken by the so-called Reformation? No; he was well aware that their supposed claim to "succession" had been the principal argument used by himself and the "Anglo-Catholic priests," to persuade Catholic Christendom to recognize them as a "living branch" of the apostolic tree.

What if he himself, and those who acted with him in bearing false witness against the true bishops of the Church, were after all only "hirelings?"

On what principle could the party to which he belonged retain their position in an establishment which utterly repudiates the idea of being any descendant in a direct line from St. Peter?

Brilliant as had been his lordship's speech in favour of the "Ecclesiastical Titles Bill," his conscience had often since reproached him for having lent his name to a mere "party cry." For he was not ignorant that the restoration of the hierarchy to England was a purely spiritual act of the head of the Church, intended for the spiritual welfare of his English subjects, and in no way affecting those outside the pale of the Catholic Church.

He also knew that so long as Catholics own no authority in spiritual matters save that of the Pope, they would most religiously cling to the titles bestowed on their bishops, spite of the notorious "Durham letter," or the thunders of Exeter Hall.

Weeks of sickness and pain had taught the Bishop of —— to mistrust the motives of himself and the "party" in the Establishment to which he belonged. Days of slow recovery had brought in their train many hours of serious reflection, during which he had compared the perfect self-abnegation which had characterised his brother Julian, and that feebleness of purpose in religious and self-aggrandizement in temporal matters, which had hitherto marked his own conduct in life.

The hand of God, in thus afflicting him, had in

mercy withdrawn the veil which, till now, had obscured his mental vision. He saw with alarm the precipice of inconsistency down which the teaching of the "Anglo-Catholic" party had driven himself, and, alas! too many others.

When once a powerful and earnest mind resolves to give up a long-cherished theory, the internal conflict may be severe, but the final issue is certain, when divine grace is brought to bear upon it. The eternal enemy of man employs at such a moment all the power of his dread kingdom; but truth finally prevails, and he who heretofore occupied the exalted position of "teacher" and "ruler" in the established Church, resolves to sit and learn, like a little child, at the footstool of an infallible authority!

Who among the brilliant throng that listened to the sweeping denunciations uttered by the Bishop of —— in the House of Lords against the Catholic religion, could have imagined that in a short time all his opinions would undergo a complete revolution? — that after months of mental agony, and going through, as an "Anglo-Catholic," every phase in the system of development, he would ultimately arrive at the conviction that if he wished to save his soul he must consent to give up earthly dignities, and submit as a mere layman to the teaching of the one Church!

CHAPTER XXVI.

On entering the library at Bankside, Mr. Horton saw at a glance that some very grave matter was engaging the "bishop's" attention. For a moment he felt half inclined to return to Lady Blanche, and tell her that he begged to decline the unpleasant task she had imposed upon him.

He experienced no particular relief as his lordship, drawing a small letter-case from his pocket, said in tones that slightly trembled, " I was on the point of sending for you, Horton, to tell you of Marion's admission into the one faith."

Mr. Horton sat as though surprise had taken away his breath. Fully anticipating an outbreak of pious anger at the news of Marion's "defection," what was his astonishment at hearing the "bishop" characterise his daughter's sad change a "return to the one faith!"

If such were the "bishop's" real opinion, it was quite within the range of probability that his lordship's own sentiments, as an "Anglo-Catholic," had recently undergone a change. And the tones of Mr. Horton's voice shook with suppressed indignation, as he replied,—

"Is it from your lips, my lord, that I hear the sad falling away of your daughter from the Church spoken of as a return to the true faith? Oh, no!" he added, in an agitated voice, "let me hear you say that in thus speaking you did but jest,—did but employ the cant phrase of those who profess to be the sole claimants to Catholicity!"

So intense a silence followed the conclusion of Mr. Horton's speech, that an almost mortal sickness seemed to take possession of his heart.

The bishop, fixing his keen eyes upon his chaplain's ashy face, at length replied, in low, clear accents,—

"No, Charles, you were not mistaken in hearing me call Marion's a return to the one faith. It is you, and I, and those who have taught the error we have done, who deserve to be told that we have all along erred, by arrogating to ourselves the name of Catholic! Who knows this better than I do? Have I not, alas! been called a champion of that sect in the establishment? Have I not taught others, and tried to persuade myself of the fable, that our peculiar teaching and pretensions entitle us to be recognized as successors of the apostles? Trace out for yourself, Charles, the effects produced by such a religious system as our Anglo-Catholic one, and discover, as I have done, the end to which it leads. Talk to the uninitiated, if you will, of the power of 'development' contained in the Church of England, and boast of the 'progress' you are making in the dishonest attempt to engraft on a Protestant establishment the doctrines taught by the one holy Catholic Church! But with me it is useless for you to employ your sophistry, as I tell you that I am fully convinced that I ought no longer to retain my false position, and call myself a bishop. I look around on the increasing evil of spiritual destitution. I see the vain efforts of our 'party' in the establishment to re-unite the people of England by the bond of a common faith. And what, let me ask, can you or I, in this wonderful nineteenth century, answer to the simple question, 'Tell me what is your rule of faith?' Again, we are told that the establishment separated from the Church of Rome on account of her supposed errors. But what errors can be more deadly than those which are now preached in the establishment,—denial of Baptismal Regeneration, disbelief in the Incarnation, and want of faith in the most blessed Presence of Jesus in the Holy Sacrament? Do not heresies like these, Charles, strike at the very foundation of Christianity? Or, can we wonder that infidelity, with giant steps, is striding over the land, and that those who are anxious to find truth should have recourse to the Church of the apostles, and humbly submit themselves to the vicar of Christ!"

"This, then," groaned poor Mr. Horton, "is the end of all my labour in the Anglo-Catholic cause, to hear from the lips of my own bishop that he, too, abandons the 'Church of his fathers,' and takes refuge in that of Rome!"

And addressing his bishop, he continued,—

"Do you not know, my lord, that it is the desertion of men like you that inflicts such fearful wounds on the Church of England? Think of the powerful example of such men as M——, and W——, and N—— going over to Rome! They went not alone. Hundreds from the ranks of the clergy and laity followed their sad defection from the Church."

"My dear Charles, if cause were wanting to convince me that in joining the Catholic Church I am taking the best means to redeem the past, your last admission would supply me with an excellent one. For, surely, if I feel that I have sinned by leading others into error, am I not bound to use the influence of my example, and endeavour to guide them to the truth? As a consistent 'Anglo-Catholic,' you cannot blame me if I join the Church of Rome, feeling, as I do, that my assumption of the title of 'bishop' has long enough placed me in a false position. It may be painful to utter a truth disagreeable to our natural pride; but it is not the less a fact, that all so-called bishops and priests of the Protestant Church are, in reality, but simple laymen in the judgment of the Catholic Church."

"Do you mean to imply, my lord, that you actually coincide with the Church of Rome in ignoring the orders of the 'Anglo-Catholic' Church, and that I, one of her 'priests,' possess no authority to consecrate?"

"Yes, Charles," was the calm reply; "I repudiate and utterly ignore the authority of any 'priest' in the Protestant Church to celebrate those sacred rites, unless he has received ordination from a regular successor of St. Peter. Indeed, what can be more absurd, my dear Charles, than to call yourself a 'priest,' when the law has decided that you can have no altar, and that it is contrary to the doctrine of the Protestant Church (to which you have sworn obedience) to teach that the celebration of the Lord's Supper is a sacrifice! Oh, believe me, Charles, the day is not distant when men of earnest minds will feel even yet more deeply than they do at the present time that, amid all this contention about doctrine, this fearful irruption of rationalism and infidelity, there is but the 'one city of refuge' to flee to,—but 'one ark of safety' to enter. Glad should I have been "—and his lordship's voice shook with emotion—" to have joined the 'household of the faith' with one so dear to me as you are. But if this blessing be denied me, I will continue to hope and pray that the lamp of faith may, in God's own time, shine upon your steps, and guide you to that Church against which 'the gates of hell shall never prevail.'"

"Deeply, my lord, as I feel for the kind wishes you have expressed in my regard, not even the consolation that your lordship would bear me company would induce me to forsake the Anglo-Catholic faith. No, say what you will of our orders, as I have lived so I hope to die a 'priest of the Church Catholic in England!' It would be fruitless for me to reason further with your lordship. So I must take a sad farewell, remembering, amidst the bitter pain of such a parting, the pleasant hours of spiritual converse we have held together, when you spoke as a faithful guardian of the 'Anglo-Catholic Church.'"

Tears started to the eyes of both bishop and chaplain, as their hands met in a last warm pressure. Each felt that never again on earth would their souls mingle in pious communion!

CHAPTER XXVII.

PEACEFULLY glided away the summer days in the quiet convent of our Lady of Mercy at Branston. The sweet notes of the Angelus bell rang clearly through the now fresh autumn air, teaching hearts weary of the world's unceasing strife and care, that in the loving mystery of our dear Lord's incarnation they may find comfort and rest for their souls.

The sons of toil began to love the cheering sound of the convent bell. " It made a body feel more cheerful-like," to hear it at their work. Prudent matrons, "on household cares intent," began to listen with an interest—hitherto a stranger to them—to the bell, which summoned the nuns to prayer, and sent on their knees the convent children, lisping the sweet " Hail, Mary."

Silently but surely the change which always takes place wherever a convent or monastery is founded was going on at Branston. Already the girls from the nuns' school were in much request as domestic servants; and not a few of the inhabitants—judging of the tree by its fruits—began to recall the visitation of the dreadful cholera, and to speak in grateful praise of the services of the Catholic bishop Julian Vavasour. And now the good seed he had sown in his great Master's vineyard began to spring up into an abundant harvest of immortal souls.

Yes, ye bigots of Exeter Hall, rail on against the ancient faith of England! You cannot shut your eyes, and those of your dupes, to the glaring fact, that no sooner is a Catholic church once built—it may be in a locality almost destitute of Catholics—than the "small grain of mustard" rapidly produces a goodly tree, sheltering hundreds beneath its branches!

Intense was the horror of Mrs. Major Smith, Miss Stellard, and their "Society for the Extinction of Roman Catholics in England, Ireland, and all over the World," when the first rumour reached their ears, that Julián Vavasour, the Catholic Bishop of Branston, had been seen to issue from the gates of Branston Court! In addition, Miss Stellard was able to inform her dear friends that he had just returned from a visit to his brother, the Bishop of ——. Improving the occasion, she exclaimed,—

"When we see popery thus exalted in the high places,—when we know that Marion and Francis Vavasour have both fallen victims to those enemies in disguise, the Jesuits, what security have we that our bishop will escape the deadly snare?"

Alas for the peace of these pious-minded ladies, whose special vocation in this world seems to consist in looking after the souls which need not their care, and neglecting those, it may be, living in the bosom of their own families in the gross neglect of all Christian duties! Alas for their serenity, had they been aware of the struggle that was taking place in the mind of the Bishop of ——, between his religious convictions and the difficulty of resigning his position as a spiritual peer in the Protestant establishment! To resign his see whilst yet perfectly able to perform its duties, was to take a step without a precedent in the records of the State Church. But, to give up such a coveted position, to become a mere layman in the Church of Rome, would, he was well aware, draw down upon him the anger of the prime minister to whom he owed his appointment, and expose him to the fierce scorn of all parties in the Establishment. Well he knew that he was at perfect liberty to believe and teach the rankest Socinianism, the most ultra Rationalism, the most extreme Calvinism, provided always he continued a member of that religious system which supplies, in these days, so apt an illustration of the "house divided against itself."

But let him once attempt to exercise this much-boasted Protestant liberty, by becoming a Catholic, and no one knew better than his lordship the natural result of such an experiment. A man less in earnest would long hesitate ere he brought down upon his own head the anger and bigotry of a whole nation.

But Francis Vavasour, " Bishop " of ——, was not the man to hesitate when he had once made up his mind that a path of duty lay before him. Being now fully convinced that in the Church of Rome alone was to be found the precious " pearl of truth," he at once resolved to " sell all and purchase it."

The words, " Thou shalt not bear false witness against thy brother," heard on the eventful night of the celebrated " Ecclesiastical Titles " debate, now led him to seek an interview with that brother from whom, years back, he had separated with coldness, for having taken that very path which he himself was now on the eve of following!

The moment Miss Stellard observed the Catholic Bishop of Branston emerge from the lodge-gates of Bankside was immediately after the first affecting interview between the long-estranged brothers.

Very rarely had the face of one of the brothers worn an expression of greater joy than it did at that happy meeting! Strong as was his faith in the marvellous effects produced by prayer, it was no easy matter for him to realize the idea that the brother for whose conversion he had never ceased to ask daily before the altar was actually prepared to resign all that the world most values, become a simple layman, and submit in the spirit of a little child to the teaching of an infallible authority! Tears of joy, such as angels might be supposed to shed at the conversion of a sinner, yet glittered in his eyes, as, hastening into the beautiful church of the Immaculate Conception, he prostrated himself before the altar of the most Blessed Sacrament. With head lowly bent upon his hands, earth, with its joys and sorrows, gradually faded before him, while contemplating the wondrous mercies of redeeming love thus inviting those who "labour and are heavy burdened" to come and draw, from the fount of His sacred heart, the living waters of joy and gladness.

CHAPTER XXVIII.

Christmas, that most joyous season of the year, has come, and the magnificent old hall at Branston Court is decked, as of yore, with the bright green and red of the cheerful holly. The drive to the avenue is covered with the rapidly-falling snow.

But on the hearts of Sir Thomas and Miss Freeman has fallen a colder blight than any of those bitter frosts which have cut off the flowers in the garden, and icebound the lake in the deer park! For the sentence of death has gone forth; and on the holy day which brought peace into the world, it is known to all the afflicted household that the fairest flower of Branston is withering rapidly beneath the malignant influence of decline!

Even in the servants' hall voices are hushed, and tears are seen in the eyes of many of the old retainers, as they talk of their sweet young mistress, lying at that festive time on her bed of death!

And to Edith herself had the weary months brought no change? Had she no pang at parting with the tried friends of her life, that she could lay thus calmly, as if, indeed, she had already passed beyond the confines of this world of pain.

Yes, Edith was indeed changed; but, as the bud is changed by the sun's warm light into the perfect beauty of the opened flower. That which appeared to the spectators but the deathbed of a young girl in the first sweet dawn of life was to Edith the grand approach to the haven of eternal rest. Like those bright lamps, wreathed in flowers, which are sent floating down the sacred stream of the Indus, and which disappear when they reach the centre of those mighty waters, so life's taper, when lit from the lamp of faith, will continue to burn brightly until it approaches the great ocean of eternity.

Edith was changed, as are those loving souls to whom Jesus gives peace. And He has also given her faith, for she is now a child of His One, Holy, Catholic Church.

Mary, the Immaculate Mother of God, is also her Mother, the saints and angels are interceding in her behalf, and, to crown all, our Blessed Lord has given himself to her on this peaceful Christmas Day! Thus, her every thought filled with love for her Saviour and her God, and pressing to her flattering heart the image of the crucified One, it is better to speak of Edith not as on a bed of death, but rather on a bed of life, the eternal life of the soul.

Early in the commencement of what she felt would be her last illness, Edith had written for the Catholic Bishop, Julian Vavasour. Her mind experienced no feeling of security when she was attending those daily services in the restored church of which Mr. Horton was the " priest."

There was an evident unreality about those Anglo-Catholic devotions, that did not satisfy the genuine piety of her heart. So she soon ceased to attend Mr. Horton's pretty church, and much to that worthy "priest's" annoyance, the pony-chair of the heiress of Branston Court might often be seen standing at the massive door of the convent of our Ladye of Mercy.

The severe trial which had visited her young heart, served to purify it from earthly affections, and gradually prepare her soul for the solemn change that awaited her.

The sweet lessons of holiness acquired in her daily visits to the convent had served as so many sign-posts along the road of perfection, directing her steps over the narrow, but royal way of the Cross.

Hence, on that bright festival of "Peace on earth to men of goodwill," the young heiress of Branston Court lay in calm repose, with a feeling of inward joy such as few experience, waiting for the heavenly messenger, whose coming she hoped would be to her the glad summons to eternal bliss.

Ah! would that all could thus wait in holy resignation, strengthened by the reception of the sacraments! Would that all could thus testify to their love for Him who died for their redemption! Would that every thought and action of our lives could tend to increase the honour and glory due to the most Precious Blood shed for us, so that even our death might bear testimony to the sincerity of our belief in the holy faith we have professed during our lives!

The last rays of the setting sun on that glorious Christmas Day, falling on the head of the dying girl, threw round it a halo as it were of immortality! No sound broke the stillness of that chamber of death, save the gasping sobs which, from time to time, escaped the grief-laden hearts of poor Sir Thomas and Miss Freeman. Kneeling with poor Edith's thin hands clasped in theirs, they rose only on the entrance of the Right Reverend Julian Vavasour, Father Aloysius, and the acolytes, who came for the purpose of reciting those exquisite and consoling prayers which the Church has appointed to be read over her departing children.

The last blessing has been pronounced on that soul, now fluttering, as it were, on the confines of earth and heaven. The bishop of God's Church, strong in the power of his holy office, has just given utterance to the first words of that sublime prayer, " Go forth, O Christian soul, from this world," when the short, irregular breathing of the gentle sufferer ceased to fall upon the ear; and those who knelt in pious awe around that innocent deathbed, recognized in the sweet smile which came over Edith the harbinger of a glorious immortality!

CHAPTER XXIX.

A YEAR has come and gone since the death of Edith Paget, the once lovely heiress of Branston Court. A plain marble cross, with the single letters " R. I. P.," marks the spot where she was laid, in the quiet old church of Branston. Thither often the feeble steps of poor Sir Thomas and his sister are bent, as they, too, alike children of the one blessed faith, come to kneel and pray for the eternal repose of her whose bright example led them to enter into the Church of Christ.

The snows of more than seventy winters are scattered on the venerable heads bent in prayer at the foot of that white marble emblem of a Redeemer's love. Earth, its cares and its sorrows, its hopes and joys, have ceased to interest those two mourning hearts.

Day by day, as the ancient housekeeper at Somerton Court watches, with that keen eye of affection which a life-service of fifty years is calculated to produce, the faltering steps of her beloved master and mistress going forth, arm-in-arm, to pray at the grave of their idolized ward, tears bedew the eyes of the kind-hearted Mrs. Grey. For there rises before her a vision of the old library shut up, darkened rooms, and, anon, the plumed hearse, carrying to their last resting-place in the family vault at Somerton the heart-broken Sir Thomas and Miss Freeman.

The affections of old age are so deeply rooted, that a blow once struck seldom fails to produce a mortal wound. The chords of memory no strange hand can wake again, no fresh interest can replace the lost one!

So, gently and peacefully, as the ripe fruit drops from the tree, Sir Thomas and his sister slept beneath the cross!

The fine old avenue of Branston Court was trod again by childhood's steps, and once more the old mansion rang with the echoes of a young girl's voice. For its late owner had bequeathed Branston Court to the infant daughter of Francis and Violet Vavasour; and a merry group, consisting of the young heiress and her nurse, Captain and Mrs. Vavasour, and their valued friend Mrs. Tichborne, were anxiously awaiting the arrival of the guests who were to celebrate the installation of Miss Vavasour in her recently acquired property.

No longer a mere dreamer, Captain Vavasour had remained constant to his good resolutions. He had long ceased to make society his idol, and set himself to work out in earnest the political and spiritual regeneration of his countrymen. Through the interest of the Irish Catholics he had been returned as member for the county of ——; and it was a subject of remark even among his most bitter opponents in the House of Commons that few men exhibited more zeal for the good of others than the recent favourite of the fashionable world, Captain Vavasour.

This happy change was entirely owing to two causes, viz., the divine light of faith, that made him so anxious to redeem the past, and the bright example of practical religion, exhibited in the lives of his fair young wife and Mrs. Tichborne.

The past, with all its bitter memories, was for ever blotted out from the remembrance of Violet. Or, if one painful thought passed across her mind, it instantly faded away when, kneeling before the image of the Crucified, she humbly

K

returned thanks to our dear Lord for his unspeakable mercy in restoring her husband, and uniting their hearts in a more tender affection by the bond of a common faith.

A change, which will for ever leave its traces at Bankside, has at length been made, an important step has been taken; that bugbear, the opinion of the world, has been disregarded, and, freed from the soul-galling shackles of the State Church, Francis Vavasour has resigned his see, and no longer holds the "enviable" position of Lord Bishop of —— !

From being the champion of "Anglo-Catholicity," and holding the wonderful office of a "priest" in the Protestant Church, he has made complete submission to the teaching of an infallible authority, and become a simple layman in the Catholic Church !

The burst of popular anger on the occasion, furious though it was, could not be compared to the expressions of contempt and reproach which assailed him from his late "Anglo-Catholic" party. But, to say nothing of the higher motives which prompted his resignation, Francis Vavasour felt assured that, in following up his real convictions, he had acted with far greater honesty of purpose than any of those "Anglo-Catholic priests" who raised such an outcry at his "going over to Rome."

Yes; he had manfully sat down to "count the cost," and he was ready to meet the most severe trials in defence of the precious gift of faith which God had given him. Never did child more meekly submit to the teaching of a beloved parent than did the late bishop, the once great leader of "Anglo-Catholicity," lay aside the "learning" of which he was once so proud, to be guided, step by step, in the "way of the Cross" by the instruction of his brother Julian, the real bishop of the one Catholic Church!

CHAPTER XXX.

THE sweet-toned bells of the chapel of our Ladye of Mercy were ringing a merry peal, and crowds of the inhabitants of Branston might be seen wending their way towards the great door of the convent. A ceremony, strange to most of them, was to take place that morning, but one to them of special interest, as it was the profession, as a Sister of Mercy, of Marion Vavasour, daughter of their late bishop.

Numerous lights blazed on the high altar, and the most exquisite flowers lent their brilliant aid to form a scene of holy splendour, such as appealed even to the bigoted Miss Stellard, whose curiosity had attracted her to the chapel. The rich notes of the sweet-toned organ pealed forth one of those glorious hymns whose harmonies seem to waft the entranced listener above the confines of earth far into celestial realms.

Slowly, two by two, preceded by the ensign of man's redemption, issued from the sacristy a white-robed procession of acolytes and priests, closed by the bishop, vested in a magnificent cope, and mitre glittering with precious stones. Even Miss Stellard, as she gazed in rapt astonishment, could not forbear recalling the good old Catholic times of England's truest glory.

There was a moment's pause, and then, with eyes bent humbly on the ground, came on and on, even to the very altar steps, a long line of those saintly women, whose lives, perchance for many a year, had been dedicated to the service of their great Master.

Who could gaze on those faces, on which the very peace of God seemed to shine forth, and find it in their hearts (strangers though they might be to the ancient faith) to believe or utter one word of calumny against these faithful servants of the Cross? Who can honestly believe that women, rich in the gifts of birth, of fortune, and youth, would abandon the world, and all the attractions it offers, especially to the young, unless they were powerfully actuated by the love of God, and the desire of serving Him in the persons of the poor and afflicted?

Slowly fell upon the ear of the listening multitude the thrilling melody of the sublime "Veni Creator." Sweetly blended the voices of those pure daughters of God into one harmonious strain as they invoked His richest spiritual gifts on her who was about to become His spouse.

Marion Vavasour, kneeling before the Bishop, and reverently pronouncing the solemn vows of poverty, chastity, and obedience, received from his lordship the black veil, that henceforth consecrated her to the life of a "religious."

The blessing had been given, the service was concluded, the nuns, with their new sister, had departed to their convent, and still one solitary figure knelt on, as if absorbed in earnest prayer. At length the worshipper rose from his knees, and revealed the sad pale face of the Rev. Charles Horton. An impulse stronger than his "good resolution" had attracted him to the chapel, in order to witness the ceremony of Marion's profession. He could scarcely even yet realize the truth that she was indeed a "spouse of Christ." Strong feelings were contending in his breast as he strode hastily up the village path leading to the rectory. But high above all the pleading of his better nature rose the voice of his arch enemy—pride of intellect.

Yes, spite of all the wonderful effects produced by the one Catholic Church, of which he had been a witness, he came to the conclusion that it was perfectly impossible that he, Charles Horton, the clever upholder of "Anglo-Catholicity," could be in error!

In that week's organ of the party there appeared a leading article on a brilliant and sarcastic letter of the Anglican "priest," Charles Horton, reprobating the crime of defection from the "Church of our fathers!"

Since that bright day which made Marion a Sister of Mercy, she has been walking onwards and upwards, in the narrow path of perfection— the way of the Cross.

But Charles Horton, now Dean of ——, has attained the summit of his ambition, and continues his endeavours to carry out the ideas of "union" and "development."

Yet each week he becomes more and more an object of mistrust to his Protestant co-religionists, and despite the struggles of his conscience, he is content to retain the equivocal position of "priest" in the bosom of that anomaly of religious belief, the "Anglo-Catholic" Protestant Church!

The anger of Lady Blanche is somewhat appeased against Marion for becoming a nun, as she has recently heard that the Duchess of Grantly has a niece in the same convent. And when she beholds the daily good works performed by the pious Sisters of Mercy, and when, sitting beneath the shadow of the fine old trees on the lawn of Branston Court, watching the gambols of her sweet grandchild, little Edith Vavasour, she remembers that it was good Mrs. Tichborne who restored her cherished son to happiness, even her worldly heart is softened. With a smile on her still handsome face, she declares that, " as of course all her ancestors were Catholics, 'society,' after all, can hardly be astonished that her children should return to the faith of their fathers!"

Good Mrs. Tichborne, as she kneels daily in her favourite spot before the most Blessed Sacrament, offers many an earnest prayer that this poor wandering soul may likewise find rest in the one fold of Christ. And so time goes on, and seasons succeed each other, while the Catholic Church alone continues the same " yesterday and to-day."

www.ingramcontent.com/pod-product-compliance
Lightning Source LLC
Chambersburg PA
CBHW020057170426
43199CB00009B/310